COOKING

Cajun-Creole

SONIA ALLISON

COOKING
Cajun-Creole
SONIA ALLISON

Absolute Press (Publishers)
14 Widcombe Crescent Bath BA2 6AH England

Credits

Producer Jon Croft

Assistant Producer Nicki Morris

Director Sonia Allison

Assistant Director Normal Allison

Chief Critic Simon Allison

Illustrated by Lesley Champkins

Cover Lesley Champkins

Putting words together Glyn Fowles
and Debbie Corbett
(thank you, in view of my writing)

Helpful contributions
Bejam, Tilda, Tabasco, Jim Moran
(Billingsgate), Carolyn Carvele of
Food Matters, Swan Housewares,
51–51 Restaurant, Monkey Business
Restaurant (both London),
The Montelone in New Orleans,
American Rice Council, Louisiana
Tourist Board, Fiona Gordon of First
Public Relations for always coming
up trumps.

Published by Absolute Press, 14 Widcombe Crescent, Bath, England
First published February 1989 © Sonia Allison 1989 © Lesley Champkins 1989
Filmset by Sulis Typesetting, Bath
Printed by WBC Print, Barton Manor, St. Philips, Bristol
Bound by WBC Bookbinders, Maesteg. Cover printed by Stopside Print, Bath

Dedications

To my husband always for love, tolerance, patience and devotion in sickness and in health, for richer for poorer.

To our son, Simon, for eating alligator with good grace and pretending he liked it. What greater loyalty could any mother expect!

To my own Mother for teaching me the basics of life and of food – an essentially practical and far-seeing lady who never gave up hope when others did.

To the rest of my family for being proud of my achievements, such as they are, and to Lily especially who can now make meringues!

Asides

Louisiana Cajuns speak broken French—a kind of patois or French shorthand.

The national bird of Louisiana is the big-beaked pelican and is on the state seal and flag. Louisiana is nicknamed the Pelican State.

The state flower is the beautiful magnolia (Magnolia Grandiflora) which was adopted by the Legislature in 1900.

Louisiana's counties are called parishes—the only state to do so.

The name Louisiana was dedicated to Louis the Fourteenth, King of France, by Robert de La Salle, early French explorer.

The state capital is Baton Rouge.

Climate—hot and humid, though temperature drops in the winter, January especially.

Main crops of Louisiana are corn, sugar cane, rice, sweet potatoes, citrus, mixed root and green vegetables, peppers, pecans, cotton and tobacco.

The area is 50,820 square miles and the population is around four and a half million.

Louisiana cookery "is a cosmopolitan cuisine adapted to the regional recipes whose gastronomic excellence is made possible by the variety of products of the garden and the farm, and the fish and game that abound in the Louisiana marshes and coastal waters. To the region, once inhabited by Attakapas Indians, have come from the north and east the French, the Spanish, the Acadians, the English, the Irish, the Italians, the Germans and the Jews, and up from the south the Mexicans. These groups have brought with them their culinary tastes and skills, often modified but not entirely lost as they have been applied to local delicacies". Extract from **First—you make a Roux**, published by Les Vingt Quatre Club, in 1954, for the Lafayette Museum.

Asides

"New Orleans has elevated the pleasures of cooking and consuming to highly skilled, sophisticated art forms." **Favourite New Orleans Recipes**, by Ormond, Irvine and Contin, published by the Pelican Publishing Company.

"Cajun and Creole cuisine originates from Louisiana— the home of Tabasco Sauce. These cooking styles are a melting pot of varied cultures, among them Indian, French, Spanish and African. They evolved as each new ethnic group combined the best of its own traditions with ingredients that were available locally. Tradition has it that Cajun cuisine was for poor folk and Creole for aristocrats." From a give-away leaflet called Hot Ideas for Tabasco, published in the UK.

New Orleans food: "a perfect blend of French, Spanish and Black American". Taken from a description written for a Creole Food Festival held at London's Hyatt Carlton Tower, London.

Preservation Hall is where all that jazz happens.

"Cajun comes from the word Acadian and describes a group of people who left France in the early 1600's to establish their home in Nova Scotia. In 1755, exiled by the English because they refused to pledge allegiance to the Crown, the Acadians settled in South Louisiana because it was French by population and they were welcomed. Their food style is a hearty food style, basically one pot cooking, live off the land. Cajuns are an ethnic group—their music, their lifestyle. Fun and as hearty as their food. It's excitement." Joe Cahn, The New Orleans School of Cooking.

Laissez les bons temps rouler—a Cajun expression which means let the good times roll. And they do.

First make your roux. Because so many Louisiana dishes are made with this flour and fat combination, it is one of the most widely used culinary phrases.

"Legend holds, the good and righteous in Louisiana don't go to heaven, but to the big kitchen in the sky. Glory. Halleluyah. Where the chefs are Creole, soul and Cajun and the food is always piled high. Or served in continental fashion, as you like it. Or strictly southern country style. Where there's always something bubbling on the back burner, seafood Gumbo, meat pies, red beans and rice. And always done just right.

No doubt about it, Louisiana cooking makes eating twice the pleasure, and living twice as nice. Maybe it's because of the succulent seafoods so abundant in the state: gulf trout, pompano, redfish and snapper, catfish, crab, crawfish and oysters. Fresh caught, nearby.

Or maybe it's the piquant choices of French sauces, Spanish spices, country seasonings and soul food herbs. Or could it be that rare wordly spirit known to travellers as 'lagniappe'. A spirit of giving an extra pinch to the pot or a little something extra to your guests." **Louisiana, A Dream State**, published by the Louisiana Office of Tourism.

Louisiana—"it's a history with a colourful cast of characters. The Spaniard Hernando de Soto was one of the first. The Frenchman Cavalier de LaSalle claimed all of it for Louis XIV. Sieur de Bienville. Bernardo de Glavez. Henry Miller Shreve and Zachary Taylor. Andrew Jackson and the pirate Jean Lafitte. It's a crazy succession of colonial clashes and claims. In it Indian, French, Spanish, Acadian, African, Anglo and American mix and mingle, swap and trade, improvise and refine a life and culture that is unique in this country, indeed, on the face of the earth. Add to this milieu Italians, Irish, Germans, Yugoslavs and Orientals and you have some idea of how compelling the region has always been." Louisiana Office of Tourism.

Over the centuries, the differences between Cajuns and Creoles evened out and today they live harmoniously together on equal terms, sharing food, music, culture and hospitality.

"The Louisiana Native Crafts Festival is a collection of both traditional and contemporary crafts. Here one can learn to weave a rug or fry an alligator". **Le Guide, What's Happening in Acadiana**.

"In time, Creoles and Acadians intermarried and eventually almost completely absorbed the Spanish and German cultures of the area." Mrs. Bobby Potts, **Cookin' on the Mississippi**.

"Longfellow's poem of Evangeline was drawn from the story of the Acadians' troubled journey to their new homes and the separations that occurred." Mrs. Bobby Potts, **Cookin' on the Mississippi**.

The thing to do is take a paddle steamer on the Lower Mississippi, listen to the heady sounds of jazz, sip Southern Comfort in style.

"New Orleans is Deep South with a vengeance. The accent drips with molasses and the smell of magnolia is thick in the air." Renate Kohler, Daily Mail, November 1979.

"The love of Cajun Cookery dates back almost three hundred years, to a time when Louisiana stretched from the Gulf of Mexico to the border of what is now Canada. It was a time when the culture of Louisiana was a melting pot for the people who settled here . . . French, Spanish, Africans, West Indians and Americans. From this melting pot evolved what is recognised as one of the most distinct and favourable cooking styles in the world—Cajun.

Whereas Creole food was the sophisticated city food of New Orleans, based on the French culinary techniques applied to local delicacies, Cajun was the cookery of the rugged people who then lived in the bayous of Acadiana—the waterways and swamps that dot Louisiana. These people lived off the land, being mostly trappers or fishermen, and cooked their daily catch in a big black iron pot over an open fire. It was hearty, robust cookery". From a paper put out by J. C. Autin, makers of spices.

"The word Creole is a French corruption of a Spanish word and means child or children of the colony. Creoles were originally of French stock but were New Orleans native born. The Creole food style . . . is a mixture of every ethnic group that has ever been in the city of New Orleans including Indian, French, Spanish and African cuisine. Creole is a life style, a people, it's New Orleans." Joe Cahn.

Scenario

Soups, Gumbos and Jambalayas

Cajun Butter Bean Soup

A warm wonder in Acadian style, you must make this soup on cold winter days for insulation. I have compromised and used inexpensive cans of butter beans instead of uncooked ones for speed; also bacon pieces for economy. The whole thing is a thrifty and wholesome brew and can be further improved by the addition of a ham bone if you have one spare.

SERVES 8

**2 tblsp salad oil
125g (4oz) onions, peeled and chopped
125g (4oz) washed red pepper, de-seeded and chopped
175g (6oz) celery, well-scrubbed and chopped
125g (4oz) streaky bacon, coarsely chopped
1 can (400g or 14oz) tomatoes
2 cans (each 425g or 15oz) butter beans
2 bay leaves
1 level tsp salt
½ tsp Tabasco or ¼ level tsp cayenne pepper
575ml (1pt) water
chopped parsley for garnishing**

1 Sizzle oil in a heavy-based and fairly large pan. Add prepared vegetables and bacon.

2 Fry over a moderate heat until just beginning to turn golden.

3 Add tomatoes and crush down against sides of pan with the back of a spoon.

4 Mix in all remaining ingredients. Bring to boil, stirring. Lower heat and cover. Simmer 45 minutes, stirring periodically.

5 Remove bay leaves, ladle into soup bowls and sprinkle parsley over each.

Bloody Mary Soup

SERVES 6 TO 8

125g (4oz) celery, broken into pieces
125g (4oz) onions, peeled and quartered
150g (5oz) washed green pepper, de-seeded and cut into pieces
25g (1oz) parsley, washed
2 level tblsp tomato purée
900ml (1½pt) tomato juice
2 level tsp salt
75ml (3 fluid oz) vodka

An unexpected knock-out, adapted from a recipe given to me by Ed Keeling, Executive Chef at the Hyatt Regency, New Orleans. Smallish portions only as it's surprisingly fulfilling.

1 *In food processor or powerful blender, work celery, onions, pepper, parsley and tomato purée to a coarse purée.*

2 *Scrape out into a bowl and whisk in last 3 ingredients.*

3 *Ladle into soup plates or cups and add an ice cube to each.*

Crab and Sweetcorn Bisque

SERVES 8

50g (2oz) butter or
margarine
125g (4oz) onions, peeled
and grated
50g (2oz) plain flour
900ml (1½pt) warm milk
225g (8oz) fresh or canned
crabmeat
1 can (about 300g or
10½oz) cream style corn
2 to 3 level tsp salt
⅛ to ¼ level tsp cayenne
pepper
½ level tsp paprika
1 tsp Worcester sauce
275ml (½pt) single cream
8 spring onions, trimmed
and chopped
2 rounded tblsp chopped
parsley

1 Melt butter or margarine in a large saucepan. Add onions, cover and cook until soft but still pale cream in colour. It's difficult to give an exact time so peep every minute or so.

2 Stir in flour to form a roux and cook 1 minute, stirring. Gradually blend in milk. Cook, again stirring constantly, until liquid comes to the boil and thickens in the same way as a white sauce.

Bisque is a French word for a thick and creamy soup usually made with seafood. The ingredients are variable and what goes in depends entirely on the whim of the cook although the roux base (page 114) is a must. You could treat it as a meal in itself.

Point of interest

I came across this little piece on the Bisque in a brilliant paperback by Penguin, published in 1957. It is called *Plats du Jour or Foreign Food* by Patience Gray and Primrose Boyd, illustrated by David Gentleman. The book seems to me to be one of the great unknowns and I hope Penguin will revive it one day and bring pleasure to all cooks keen on history and practicalities.

"In Seventeenth-century French cookery books the bisque is a soup made of pigeons or small birds − quails, partridges − with a rich garniture. The important thing seems to have been to make the broth red, and crayfish were added to produce this effect. The crayfish finally displaced the pigeons and the bisque d'écrevisses (crayfish stewed in white wine, shelled, pounded, incorporated with crayfish butter, made from the pounded shells and claws, the whole thing passed through a sieve and reheated) held the field and the word bisque came to mean a purée of shellfish."

Crayfish bisque is made enthusiastically in New Orleans but would be prohibitively costly to emulate here.

3 Add all remaining ingredients except the last two. Cover pan and simmer Bisque gently for 15 minutes, stirring periodically.

4 Ladle into bowls and sprinkle each portion with spring onions and parsley. Serve very hot.

Gumbo

Gumbo with Seafood

SERVES 8

A typical New Orleans classic, made with a darkened roux (page 114). The flavour is distinctive, the whole thing off-beat and it must be served with the fluffiest white rice in the business – American long grain, easy-cook variety.

3 tblsp groundnut oil
50g (2oz) plain flour
225g (8oz) onions, peeled and chopped
125g (4oz) celery, well-scrubbed and thinly sliced
2 garlic cloves, peeled and crushed
125g (4oz) washed green peppers, de-seeded and chopped
2 bay leaves
2 level tsp salt
725ml (1¼pt) boiling water
½ bunch spring onions, trimmed and chopped
450g (1lb) peeled prawns, defrosted if frozen
200 to 225g (7 to 8oz) crabmeat, fresh or canned
¼ to 1 tsp Tabasco, depending on heat preferred

1 Pour oil into a saucepan. Heat until hot, add flour and cook roux 2 to 3 minutes or until it turns walnut brown. Stir almost constantly.

2 Add next 5 ingredients and cook gently, half-covered with pan lid, for ½ hour. Stir from time to time.

Gumbo is cheerfully and unmistakably African. Exotic right through and some say the national dish of Louisiana. Certainly it has won fame and acclaim in and out of the State and is categorised locally as a soup or first course, thickened with either okra (ladies' fingers) or a roux in gingersnap tan. Sometimes both but much depends on the cook who will also ladle the Gumbo into deep pottery bowls and add a mound of freshly-cooked rice to each serving. Real family stuff. No-one seems to know for sure how the name came about but it might have originated from the African quin gombo, meaning okra.

Antoine's restaurant is one of the most renowned and fashionable eating places in New Orleans and the author of the restaurant's cookbook, Roy F Guste Jr, describes Gumbo as the "Bouillabaisse of Louisiana". Yes, perhaps, but even Cajuns and Creoles sometimes skip the fish and make it regularly and successfully with chicken, pork, ham, a poultry carcass for economy and even Andouille (explained in Lagniappe) combined with fresh turkey and other meats. It works to perfection. Of course seafood is frequently used solo or added with meat and sausage. There is so much about that some of it inevitably lands in the pot ... Chunky pieces of white crabmeat, fresh and delicate oysters, pretty pink shrimps which are better known in Britain as prawns. They all add flavour and colour.

If Gumbo does relate to anything at all, then it is to a satisfying and comforting stewpot of heart-warming broth, simmered to a thick and abundantly-flavoured richness of muted greens and reds and rusts, like mellow autumn in upstate New York or Eastern Canada just before the traditional fall.

Gumbo is unsophisticated and largely unspoiled native cooking, much loved, classed as rustic and without pretensions of glamour. In no way is it an up-market eccentricity for the chosen few.

Four Comments

Okra is mucilaginous by nature and has natural thickening properties. It is classed as a vegetable and is available from some supermarkets and ethnic food shops.

The roux used in Gumbo cooking is heated until dark, like the shell of a walnut. It is quite different from the paler roux used by chefs to make classic white sauces of the French school and is used primarily to flavour and thicken Gumbos in

3 Mix in salt, water and spring onions. Bring back to boil, simmer 5 minutes and remove bay leaves. Add rest of ingredients and heat through for about 5 minutes, stirring.

4 Spoon into bowls and add rice to each.

Gumbo with Seafood and Okra

SERVES 8

Include 350g (12oz) topped, tailed and thickly sliced washed okra. Add to roux with rest of prepared vegetables. Cook 10 minutes longer.

a distinctive and individual manner.

Each portion of Gumbo should, ideally, be sprinkled with powdered sassafras leaves, known as gumbo filé or filé powder. It adds a delicate flavour, all its own. At present, the powder is not available in Britain but it will get here in its own good time and be happy to know it is not calamitous if omitted.

Before passing you over to the recipes, allow me to refer you again to Joe Cahn (New Orleans School of Cooking) who has this to say about Gumbos.

"All gumbos can be different. They can be dark, light, thin or thick. If it walks, crawls, swims, flies, slithers or stays long enough for you to grab it, you can use it in your gumbo. Gumbo is a soup dish of South Louisiana." There are three categories each with their own historical base.

Roux base

European influence. Many Cajun/Creole recipes begin with 'first make your roux.'

Okra base

African influence (African word for okra is gumbo).

Filé gumbo

Pronounced fee-lay, Red Indian influence. (Filé is in fact ground sassafras leaves. It is used to thicken a gumbo but not during cooking as it will become stringy. It should be added by each diner individually. Filé powder is not available in the UK.)

For a definition of roux, see Lagniappe section.

Chicken Gumbo

SERVES 8

**25g (1oz) butter or
margarine or 2 tblsp
salad oil
700g (1½lb) raw chicken
joints, skin removed
125g (4oz) unsmoked
gammon, cut into small
cubes
450g (1lb) okra, topped
and tailed, well washed
and cut into short lengths
450g (1lb) tomatoes,
blanched then skinned and
chopped
225g (8oz) onions, peeled
and chopped
150g (5oz) green pepper,
washed, de-seeded and
chopped
3 level tblsp finely
chopped parsley
2 small bay leaves
3 level tsp salt
2 level tsp ground
coriander
1½ level tsp turmeric
1 level tblsp tomato purée
1 litre (1¾pt) water**

*1 Sizzle butter, margarine or
oil in a large and heavy-
based pan. Add chicken
joints and gammon then fry
until both are golden brown.
This often takes longer than
you think, depending on the
source of heat, so allow
plenty of time.*

*2 Add all remaining ingredi-
ents and bring to the boil,
stirring from time to time.
Lower heat, cover pan and
cook gently for about 50
minutes or until chicken is
tender.*

*Typical of Louisiana, this Gumbo is thickened by the okra and
no additional flour is needed. It also uses some of the State's
most beloved vegetables; tomatoes, onions, celery and green
pepper, known in the US as bell pepper.*

*3 Lift out of pan, remove
meat from bones then cut
into small pieces. Return to
pan and reheat. Scoop into
bowls and add rice to each
– a good, healthy dollop or
more, depending on appetite.*

Gumbo
with Sausage

SERVES 8

*Make exactly as previous
Gumbo, adding 350g (12oz)
smoked sausage (salami
type) with the chicken. Chop
coarsely.*

Gumbo aux Herbes

SERVES 8 TO 10

450g (1lb) fresh spinach
225g (8oz) watercress
450g (1lb) iceberg lettuce
**450g (1lb) green cabbage
leaves**
2 boxes mustard and cress
1½ to 2 level tsp salt
3 tblsp peanut oil
**700g (1½lb) bacon pieces,
all fat removed**
**450g (1lb) onions, peeled
and chopped**
**2 garlic cloves, peeled and
crushed**
3 level tblsp plain flour
**2 rounded tblsp chopped
fresh parsley**
**1 rounded tblsp chopped
fresh chives**
**½ level tsp chopped fresh
sage**
**1 rounded tblsp chopped
fresh tarragon**
¼ to ½ tsp Tabasco
450ml (¾pt) boiling water

Totally different from all other Gumbos, I found this version in two books; one which I brought back with me from Louisiana called Favourite New Orleans Recipes by Ormond, Irvine and Cantin, published by Pelican in 1983. The other is from one of the finest books ever written on USA food, a Penguin Handbook by McCully, Noderer and Bullock, first published in 1964 and titled The American Heritage Cookbook. Here the authors describe the Gumbo as something which "can be made with almost any greens, seasonings and herbs. It originated in the Congo and was introduced to New Orleans by Negroes; it was then modified with herbs and sold there in the Old French market by Cherokee and Choctaw Indians." Again I have adapted the two recipes to make the version below.

1 Thoroughly wash all greens then chop up leaves and discard any tough stalks. Cut mustard and cress level to top of box.

2 Put vegetables, a handful at a time, into a large saucepan. Gently cook down, without additional water, before adding the next batch. When all the vegetables have been added, season with salt and cook steadily but moderately for 1 hour. Leave pan uncovered and stir periodically.

3 Meanwhile, heat oil in another saucepan until hot. Add bacon and quickly fry until lightly browned. Remove to a plate.

4 Add onions and garlic to remaining oil in pan then fry until golden. Mix in flour and cook, stirring, for 2 to 3 minutes or until it looks tan coloured.

5 Mix in all remaining ingredients then bring to boil, stirring all the time. Combine with greens, heat until hot and serve with rice.

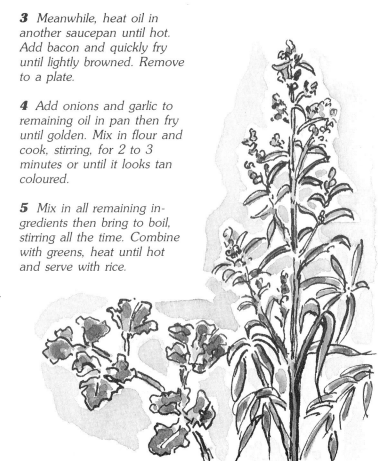

Duck Gumbo

Special occasion treatment for duck, "stretching" an expensive bird to its full capacity to give you a classic Gumbo with a touch of luxury and a bounty of onions.

SERVES 8 TO 10

6 duck joints, skinned and with fat removed
50g (2oz) dripping or margarine
50g (2oz) plain flour
2 bunches spring onions, trimmed and chopped
350g (12oz) onions, peeled and chopped
125g (4oz) celery, well-scrubbed and chopped
2 to 3 level tsp salt
1.2 litres (2pt) boiling water
½ tsp Tabasco
25g (1oz) parsley, chopped

1 Wash and dry duck. Sizzle dripping or margarine in a large, shallow pan.

2 Add duck, fry on both sides until crisp and golden. Remove to a plate and set aside temporarily.

3 Stir flour into fat in pan to form a roux. Fry over a low heat for about 3 minutes or until gingersnap brown. Stir constantly.

4 Add prepared vegetables. Cook, stirring periodically, for 5 minutes.

5 Season with salt then add water with Tabasco and parsley. Replace duck and mix in well. Simmer gently for 1 hour.

6 Remove duck from pan and take meat from bones. Cut into small pieces then return to pan.

7 Reheat until piping hot then spoon into bowls. Add freshly cooked rice to each.

Jambalaya

SERVES 4

50g (2oz) butter or margarine or 4 tblsp salad oil
225g (8oz) onions, peeled and chopped
225g (8oz) well-washed celery, thinly sliced
225g (8oz) well-washed red and green peppers (bell peppers), de-seeded and chopped
2 garlic cloves, peeled and crushed
225g (8oz) long grain rice
1 can (400g or 14oz) tomatoes
450g (1lb) cooked chicken, sausage or other cooked meats, cut into strips or small dice
225ml (8 fluid oz) boiling water
2 to 3 level tsp salt

1 Heat fat or oil in a heavy pan until hot. Add onions, celery, peppers and garlic.

2 Stir in rice, tomatoes, chicken, water and salt. Bring to boil, crushing tomatoes against sides of pan.

3 Lower heat and cover. Simmer gently for about 15 minutes or until rice is fluffy and tender and has absorbed all the liquid.

4 If it seems to be drying out too much, add tablespoon by tablespoon of boiling water. Stir round, spoon on to warm plates and serve straight away. A salad goes well.

Associated with New Orleans in much the same way as Gumbo, Jambalaya is a colourful rice mix strongly influenced by Spain's Paella. It is a brilliant way of using up cooked foods, introducing fresh ones and marrying them all together in a sturdy saucepan for a one-pot meal. The derivation of the name is obscure but may have something to do with jambon, French for ham, or from the Provencale jambalai, which refers to a dish of chicken and rice. Still on the subject of names, Joe Cahn, of the New Orleans School of Cooking, has a further explanation: "The exact translation of Jambalaya is as follows, Jamba, gift, La, with, ya, rice – Gift with rice. A one pot dish, it is a melting pot of ethnic culture. Therefore, combinations can include fish, fowl, sausage, etc". It was originally slave food in common with the Gumbo, and dates back to the 18th Century.

Jambalaya with Seafood

Make as Jambalaya, substituting 450g (1lb) peeled prawns for the chicken etc.

Jambalaya with Mixed Seafood and Ham

Make as Jambalaya but omit chicken etc. Add instead a mixture of seafood; bottled mussels (drained), smoked oysters, canned and flaked tuna, flaked smoked mackerel and about 125g (4oz) top quality ham, cut into small cubes.

Consideration

225g (8oz) peeled and diced aubergines may be added to any of the Jambalayas along with the other vegetables.

Fish

Prawn Boulettes

MAKES 20 to 40

175g (6oz) fresh white or
brown bread, cubed
50g (2oz) onions, peeled
and coarsely chopped
6 spring onions trimmed
and coarsely chopped
1 garlic clove, peeled
450g (1lb) prawns, thawed
if frozen and well-drained
½ level tsp salt
1 tsp Worcester sauce
2 to 3 drops Tabasco
1 grade 2 egg, beaten
2 level tblsp flour
extra flour for coating
deep oil for frying

An attractive cocktail savoury or light, snacky lunch, the Prawn Boulettes can be rolled into medium or small balls, depending on how they are going to be treated afterwards. For cocktails, make 40 small Boulettes and spear them on to sticks; for lunch, make larger ones and accompany with Remoulade Sauce (pages 63/64), plain mayonnaise dressed up with finely chopped black olives, or tomato ketchup hotted up with a few shakes of Tabasco. The Boulettes are just as appetising cold with salad, especially the potato one on page 78. Or a leafy green one tossed with a zesty French dressing and sprinkled with one of Louisiana's favourite herbs − chopped parsley.

Prawns or similar seafood in the Deep South are drier than our frozen or canned varieties and so I have had to use more breadcrumbs to bind. A food processor or mincing machine would be a help as it produces a smoother consistency.

1 Mince or process the bread, onions (both kinds), garlic and prawns.

2 Tip into a bowl and work in seasonings, egg and the flour. Refrigerate, covered, for 30 minutes.

3 Coat a piece of foil fairly thickly with flour. Divide prawn mixture into 20 or 40 pieces. Roll in flour.

4 Heat oil until hot. Add Boulettes, four or five at a time. Fry until golden brown and crisp-looking.

5 Remove from pan and drain on kitchen paper towels.

23

Mirliton and Prawn Gratin

SERVES 4

2 mirlitons (see page 57)
boiling salted water
2 tblsp olive or other
salad oil
125g (4oz) celery, scrubbed
and chopped
50g (2oz) onion, peeled
and chopped
125g (4oz) washed green
pepper, de-seeded and
chopped
1 garlic clove, peeled and
sliced
1 can (400g or 14oz)
tomatoes, crushed
1 level tsp salt
400g (14oz) frozen and
defrosted prawns
75g (3oz) Cheddar cheese,
grated
50g (2oz) fresh white
breadcrumbs

Topped with the almost forgotten breadcrumbs and grated cheese mix we used to call au gratin before the advent of Nouvelle Cuisine when it virtually disappeared, this casserole has turned out to be a reviver of happy memories, perfect with yellow cornbread, an easy treat for any time of year.

1 Well grease a round heat-proof dish measuring 18cm in diameter by 8cm in depth (7½ by 3 inches).

2 Peel and halve mirlitons, remove large seeds and cut flesh into chunks. Par-boil in boiling salted water for 15 minutes. Drain and dice.

3 Heat oil in a pan. Add celery, onion, green pepper and garlic. Fry gently, uncovered, for 7 minutes.

4 Mix in tomatoes and salt. Bring to boil, cover and simmer for 25 minutes.

5 Stir in prawns and mirliton dice, heat through 5 minutes then transfer to prepared dish.

6 Mix together cheese and crumbs. Sprinkle thickly over prawn mixture. Reheat and brown under hot grill for 5 to 10 minutes.

7 Served with baby new potatoes or freshly boiled rice. A salad also goes well.

Devilled Crab

**4 crab shells, well-washed
and dried or 4 scallop
shaped glass dishes
50g (2oz) butter or
margarine
50g (2oz) onion, peeled
and grated
2 level tsp plain flour
150ml (¼pt) single cream
1 level tsp Dijon mustard
1 tsp Worcester sauce
1 tblsp dry sherry or
Bourbon
2 tblsp water
1 to 1½ level tsp salt
⅛ tsp cayenne pepper
1 level tblsp finely
chopped parsley
450g (1lb) crabmeat (light
and dark), thawed if frozen
25g (1oz) Cheddar cheese,
finely grated
2 level tsp Parmesan
cheese
2 level tblsp toasted
breadcrumbs**

Cornish summers come vividly to mind when, on self-catering holidays, we would be up at the crack of dawn to collect freshly cooked crabs from our nearest fishing village and eat them just as they were the same evening for supper. The thought of doing anything to that sweet and delicate flesh would have been considered sacrilege. Times change, so do we and I've taken to devilling crabs in the same way as they do in New Orleans. They're delicious and more filling than you realise.

1 *Brush shells or dishes lightly with melted butter, oil or margarine. Set oven to 220°C (425°F), Gas 7.*

2 *Heat butter or margarine in a pan until just beginning to foam. Mix in onions and fry until just beginning to turn pale gold. Don't allow to brown.*

3 *Mix in flour to form a roux and cook 1 minute. Gradually stir in cream, mustard, Worcester sauce, sherry or Bourbon, water, salt, pepper and parsley.*

4 *Bring slowly to boil, simmer 2 minutes then fork in the crab. If mixture is too thick at this stage for personal taste, add 2 or 3 tablespoons hot water. Simmer 3 minutes.*

5 *Pile into shells or dishes. Mix together the two cheeses and crumbs then sprinkle over. Reheat and brown in the oven for 10 to 15 minutes. A lettuce salad, any kind, to accompany.*

Crab au Gratin

SERVES 8

40g (1½oz) butter or margarine
40g (1½oz) plain flour
275ml (½pt) warm milk
275ml (½pt) single cream
175g (6oz) Cheddar cheese, grated
1 tsp Worcester sauce
1 level tsp salt
¼ to ½ level tsp cayenne pepper
½ level tsp paprika
450g (1lb) crabmeat
pepper to taste
2 tblsp medium sherry
4 rounded tblsp fresh white breadcrumbs

An extravagant Cajun confection which is basically crab in a zippy cheese sauce, crispened on top with breadcrumbs and flashed under the grill. It is cooked in individual ramekin dishes and served as an appetizer with fingers of hot toast.

1 Melt butter or margarine in a saucepan. Stir in flour to form a roux and cook 1 minute.

2 Gradually blend in milk and cream. Cook, stirring, until sauce comes to the boil and thickens. Add cheese and heat gently to melt.

3 Add all remaining ingredients except crumbs. Reheat, stirring all the time, until mixture is very hot.

4 Transfer to 8 buttered ramekin dishes, sprinkle with crumbs and brown under the grill. A garnish of parsley wouldn't come amiss.

Crab Soufflé

With France written all over it, this is a classic fish soufflé which belongs to the great restaurants of New Orleans and wealthy plantation families with resident or daily cooks. It is light, soft and piquant, just the thing to go with lightly cooked green vegetables. It is also quite easy to make at home provided you have the patience.

SERVES 4

50g (2oz) butter or margarine
50g (2oz) plain flour
275ml (½pt) milk, heated to lukewarm
1 level tsp French mustard
½ to 1 level tsp salt
shake of Tabasco
½ tsp Worcester sauce
3 grade 2 eggs, separated
175 to 200g (6 to 7oz) crabmeat

1 Set oven to 190°C (375°F), Gas 5. Well grease a 1.2 litre (2 pint) straight-sided soufflé dish.

2 Melt butter or margarine in a saucepan. Stir in flour to form a roux and cook 1 minute.

3 Gradually blend in milk and cook, stirring all the time, until mixture forms a thick sauce.

4 Work in next 4 ingredients with egg yolks and crabmeat. Beat whites to a very stiff snow, adding a pinch of salt or cream of tartar for extra bulk.

5 Gently fold into crab mixture with a large metal spoon. When all streakiness has disappeared, spoon into prepared dish.

6 Bake 45 minutes without opening the oven door. Eat straight away by spooning out on to plates – a soufflé falls as you watch it.

Congealed Crab Salad

SERVES 8

1 sachet powdered gelatine
3 tblsp cold water
150ml (¼pt) tomato juice
1 tblsp Worcester sauce
150ml (¼pt) soured cream
2 rounded tblsp mayonnaise
1½ level tsp salt
strained juice of ½ a large lemon
1 can (170g) crab in brine, drained
1 large hard boiled egg, peeled and chopped
150g (5oz) onions, peeled and finely chopped
75g (3oz) celery, well-washed and finely chopped

1 Tip gelatine into a saucepan. Add water and soak 1½ minutes. Melt over minimal heat.

2 Stir in next six ingredients. Flake up crab and add to gelatine mixture with egg, onions and celery.

3 Rinse a 1.2 litre (2 pint) plain or fluted mould with cold water.

4 Spoon in the crab salad and set in the refrigerator overnight or until firm.

5 Unmould, cut into 8 portions and arrange over lettuce-lined plates.

Congealed is a lovely, old-fashioned and descriptive word some U.S. cookery writers still use when talking about any dish set with jelly. This one is a popular starter; rich, creamy and briskly-flavoured, stunning with a salad of iceberg lettuce or Webb's Wonder.

Congealed White Fish Salad

Make as the Crab Salad, but substitute 175g (6oz) cooked and flaked white fish for the crab.

Congealed Salmon Salad

An adaptation for Britain.
Make as the Crab Salad, but substitute 1 can (200g or 7oz) red salmon for the crab. Drain salmon and flake up flesh.

Congealed Tuna Salad

Make as the Crab Salad, but substitute 1 can (200g or 7oz) tuna for the crab. Drain tuna and coarsely mash up flesh.

Congealed Prawn Salad

Make as the Crab Salad, but substitute 175g (6oz) peeled and chopped prawns for the crab.

Oysters Rockefeller

SERVES 4

**50g (2oz) butter or
margarine
25g (1oz) spring onions,
trimmed and very finely
chopped
50g (2oz) frozen chopped
spinach, partially thawed
25g (1oz) parsley, finely
chopped
2 level tblsp very finely
chopped celery leaves
2 large lettuce leaves, very
finely chopped
40g (1½oz) dried
breadcrumbs
1 tblsp Pernod or Ricard
½ level tsp salt
5 drops Tabasco
1 tsp Worcester sauce
½ level tsp bottled
anchovy essence (optional)
2 tblsp double cream
pinch of ground bay leaves
16 large oysters on the
half shell
rock salt**

1 Set oven to 220°C
(425°F), Gas 7.

2 Heat butter or margarine
in a pan until it is just
beginning to sizzle. Add
spring onions and fry 3
minutes over medium heat.

3 Stir in spinach, parsley,
celery leaves and lettuce.
Continue to fry gently for 5
minutes. Add all remaining
ingredients except oysters and
salt. Leave aside temporarily.

*Britain has some of the finest oysters in the Western world
which take naturally to being Rockefellered à la New Orleans.
Although oysters abound in Louisiana, this recipe is a very
special production and was first created in 1899 by Jules
Alciatore, proprietor of Antoine's, the restaurant immortalised
by Frances Parkinson Keyes in her novel, Dinner at Antoine's.
It has French chic and Southern stamina but the original recipe
remains a secret and no-one knows, apart from the restaurant
chefs, exactly what goes into the green topping. All I can tell
you is that it is quite rich and flavoured with Pernod or Ricard,
whichever is available. As no other recipe can claim to be
authentic, we food writers have to be content with our own
versions. This is mine.*

4 Cover base of a shallow,
medium baking tin (like a
Swiss roll tin) with salt to
keep oyster shells in place
and prevent them from
toppling over.

5 Gently, using a teaspoon,
pile topping mixture over
each oyster. Bake 10 minutes
then serve straight away,
allowing 4 per person.

Consideration
*If oysters are small, use
double the quantity.*

Blackened Cooking (Red fish)

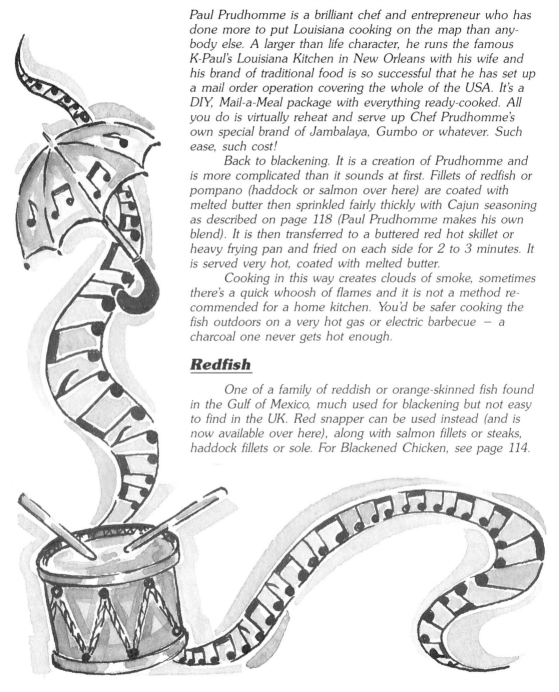

Paul Prudhomme is a brilliant chef and entrepreneur who has done more to put Louisiana cooking on the map than anybody else. A larger than life character, he runs the famous K-Paul's Louisiana Kitchen in New Orleans with his wife and his brand of traditional food is so successful that he has set up a mail order operation covering the whole of the USA. It's a DIY, Mail-a-Meal package with everything ready-cooked. All you do is virtually reheat and serve up Chef Prudhomme's own special brand of Jambalaya, Gumbo or whatever. Such ease, such cost!

Back to blackening. It is a creation of Prudhomme and is more complicated than it sounds at first. Fillets of redfish or pompano (haddock or salmon over here) are coated with melted butter then sprinkled fairly thickly with Cajun seasoning as described on page 118 (Paul Prudhomme makes his own blend). It is then transferred to a buttered red hot skillet or heavy frying pan and fried on each side for 2 to 3 minutes. It is served very hot, coated with melted butter.

Cooking in this way creates clouds of smoke, sometimes there's a quick whoosh of flames and it is not a method recommended for a home kitchen. You'd be safer cooking the fish outdoors on a very hot gas or electric barbecue – a charcoal one never gets hot enough.

Redfish

One of a family of reddish or orange-skinned fish found in the Gulf of Mexico, much used for blackening but not easy to find in the UK. Red snapper can be used instead (and is now available over here), along with salmon fillets or steaks, haddock fillets or sole. For Blackened Chicken, see page 114.

Tail Pieces

Trout Amandine

A Louisiana term to describe what we know better as trout and almonds. Often the trout is filleted and requires less cooking time.

Aubergine Casserole with Seafood

SERVES 6

Make as Aubergine Casserole with Beef (page 38) but substitute 450g (1lb) prawns or crab for the beef. Mix into fried vegetables at the same time as the mashed aubergines and don't fry any further or fish will toughen.

Cajun 'Popcorn'

SERVES 6

A term to describe prawns which have been sprinkled with Cajun seasoning (page 118) then coated in batter and deep-fried. They are treated in New Orleans as a hot snack or starter and go well with the mayonnaise-based Remoulade sauce on pages 63/64. The sauce is improved by the addition of a teaspoon or two of medium sherry.

Fried Catfish

I wonder how often people fry fish at home these days when fish and chip shops abound and packs of ready-coated or battered fish can be grilled, baked or microwaved instead.

Down in the South they still fry regularly, choosing locally farmed catfish fillets which are coated in egg and cornmeal. The fish looks like any other small white fish and the nearest here would be filleted whiting, pieces of haddock or young cod. Almost anything goes, provided Hush Puppies (page 84) accompany!

Crawfish Boil

I can only tell you about this ritualistic feast because the cost of crawfish (crayfish), used in the sort of quantities considered normal in Louisiana, would render most of us bankrupt.

About 2 or 3 kilogrammes of crawfish are boiled at a time in well-seasoned water containing salt (added towards the end) pepper, sliced lemon, garlic and bay leaves. Potatoes and sweetcorn ears are also included (tied in a cloth for ease of removal) which are eaten with the crawfish. Cooking time is about 15 minutes, the crawfish are drained and then left to sit in the pot, tightly covered, for about 5 minutes. Afterwards they are tipped out on to a table lined with newspaper – plates if you're lucky! It's then finger food all the way and no dignity expected.

Crabs and Crawfish

More experiences from Ed Keeling, Executive Chef at the Hyatt Regency, New Orleans.

Soft Shell Crabs

(allow 2 to 3 per person) These cost the earth in Britain, about £1.60 each at the last count, and are about twice the size of a large spider. They have soft shells, hence the name, and are eaten claws and all. To prepare, "wash and clean bottom, remove sex organs and clean under wings". Good luck! The next step is to coat them in thick batter, roll in cornmeal and deep fry.

Soft Shell Crawfish

I'm not too sure about the sex organs this time but you have to pinch off heads before coating with flour and cornmeal prior to deep-frying.

Tail Pieces

Etouffée of Seafood

SERVES 8

Prepare the same selection of vegetables as used in the Beef Daube (page 41) and fry in 50g (2oz) butter or margarine. Blend in 25g (1oz) flour, 275ml (½pt) water and 1 can (400g or 14oz) crushed tomatoes. Bring to boil, stirring. Lower heat, cover and simmer 30 minutes. Add 450g (1lb) cooked seafood (fresh, canned or frozen and thawed). Reheat and serve.

Shrimp Creole

SERVES 6

A whizz kid with style and even featured on a New Orleans postcard — that's fame for you!

Make up one and a half times the Creole sauce on page 62, adding 3 blanched and chopped tomatoes. Heat until bubbly then mix in 1kg (2lb) raw jumbo prawns, shelled first. Simmer until shrimps turn pink which could take anything from 5 to 7 minutes. Serve with freshly cooked rice.

Mahi-Mahi

An exotic warm water fish with white flesh and a skin that is silvery-grey and tinged with pale yellow. It is also covered with small dark spots. It looks like a small haddock and is often called dolphin fish though it is not related to the dolphin. It is mild in flavour, not wildly exciting and best fried or grilled. It cries out for Creole sauce (page 62).

Shrimp Remoulade

SERVES 4 TO 6

One of the all time favourites in Louisiana, this is the Southern version of our own prawn cocktail.

Make up Remoulade sauce (2) as directed on page 64. Toss in 450 to 700g (1 to 1½lb) peeled prawns. Cover and refrigerate until thoroughly chilled. Spoon on to lettuce-lined plates or put into glasses, one-third filled with shredded lettuce.

Meat, Poultry
and Game

Meat Balls in Tomato Sauce

SERVES 4 TO 6

Sauce
2 tblsp salad oil
175g (6oz) onions, peeled and chopped
1 can condensed tomato soup
1 can (400g or 14oz) sieved Italian tomatoes
1 level tsp salt
1 level tsp basil
1 tblsp wine or cider vinegar
½ level tsp cinnamon
150ml (¼pt) water

Meat Balls
700g (1½lb) beef for braising or very lean mince
1 level tsp mixed herbs
125g (4oz) fresh white or brown breadcrumbs
1 clove garlic, crushed
2 Grade 2 eggs, beaten
2 level tblsp chopped parsley
3 level tblsp grated Parmesan cheese (optional)

For Serving
350g (12oz) freshly cooked spaghetti
grated Parmesan cheese

1 For sauce, heat oil in a large, deep frying pan until sizzling. Add onions, cover pan and fry gently until pale gold.

2 Mix in all remaining ingredients. Bring to boil, stirring constantly as tomatoes have a tendency to stick. Cover and leave to simmer while preparing meat balls.

Characterfully Italian, this is much loved in Louisiana where it is served with spaghetti and grated Parmesan cheese. My recipe is a short cut one but it hasn't come to any harm on the way. The art, if there is such a thing with meat balls, is to use lean, lean mince and to this end I generally buy braising steak and run it through the food processor.

3 Put beef into a deep dish. Using your hands, work in herbs, crumbs, garlic, eggs, parsley and Parmesan if used.

4 Shape into 12 balls with dampened hands. Arrange in pan of sauce in a single layer.

5 Spoon sauce over top of meat balls, cover with lid and simmer 45 minutes.

6 Arrange on top of spaghetti (50 to 75g or 2 to 3oz per person) and sprinkle with parsley.

Consideration
Chopped spring onions can be used with parsley for sprinkling. Allow about 6 medium ones.

Meat Loaf Cajun Style (1)

SERVES 6 TO 8

**700g (1½lb) lean minced
beef
225g (8oz) minced pork or
raw minced turkey
2 tblsp oil
125g (4oz) onions, peeled
and finely chopped
6 spring onions, trimmed
and finely chopped
75g (3oz) celery, scrubbed
and finely chopped
1 garlic clove, peeled and
crushed
150g (5oz) washed green
pepper, de-seeded and
chopped
2 tsp molasses
2 level tblsp tomato purée
½ to 1 tsp Tabasco (cut
down if you prefer less
fire)
50g (2oz) fresh white
breadcrumbs
2 grade 2 eggs, beaten
1 to 1½ level tsp salt**

One of the great pleasures of Louisiana cooking, Meat Loaf is basic, earthy, rustic and economical; a tower of strength with Creole or Mushroom sauce (pages 62/70) and rice. No pretensions of grandeur here at all, no childish behaviour, no tantrums, no disappointments, just soul food to warm the everyday heart when the first touch of frost nips the air. A gladsome thing.

1 Put both meats into a bowl and knead together with dampened hands.

2 Sizzle oil in a frying pan. Add next 5 ingredients and fry gently for 12 minutes, over a lowish heat, until soft and just beginning to turn golden.

3 Work into both meats with all remaining ingredients. Again knead thoroughly with dampened hands and shape into 20 by 10cm (8 by 4 inch) loaf.

4 Transfer to a piece of greased foil lining a baking tray and cook 1¼ hours in oven set to 180°C (350°F), Gas 4.

5 Cut into slices and serve. If there are any leftovers, slice and use in sandwiches or eat cold with salad.

Cajun Meat Loaf (2)

SERVES 6 TO 8

450g (1lb) lean minced beef
225g (8oz) pork sausage meat
125g (4oz) onions, peeled and grated
75g (3oz) celery, well-scrubbed and very finely chopped
65g (2½oz) white bread, cubed
125ml (4 fluid oz) hot milk
1 grade 1 or 2 egg, beaten
¼ tsp Tabasco
1 level tsp salt
1 level tsp dried thyme
1 level tsp French mustard

A novelty meat loaf concocted from minced beef and pork sausage meat. It's a good thing to have around, economical, herby, bright as a button and a perfect partner for Creole sauce. In Louisiana the obvious accompaniment would be rice — here potatoes perhaps.

1 Knead together beef and sausage meat with dampened hands. Work in onions and celery.

2 Put bread into a bowl. Add milk. Soak for 5 minutes then gradually beat in egg. Work into meat mixture thoroughly.

3 Fork in Tabasco, salt, thyme and mustard. Shape into a 20 by 10 cm (8 by 4 inch) loaf.

4 Transfer to a piece of greased foil lining a baking tray and cook 1¼ hours in oven set to 180°C (350°F), Gas 4.

5 Serve as Meat Loaf Cajun Style 1 (page 35).

Kibby

SERVES 8 TO 10

575ml (1pt) boiling water
250g (9oz) kibbled wheat
(bulgar)
350 to 400g (12 to 14oz)
lean minced beef
75g (3oz) onion, peeled
and coarsely chopped
1 level tsp salt
1 level tsp paprika
½ level tsp black pepper
¼ level tsp allspice

Filling
1 tblsp salad oil
175g (6oz) onions, peeled
and grated
350g (12oz) lean minced
beef
1 level tsp salt
75g (3oz) pine nuts, lightly
toasted under the grill

Topping
50g (2oz) butter or
margarine, melted

1 Well grease a dish measuring 20 by 23cm (about 8 by 9 inches).

2 Pour water into a bowl. Stir in kibbled wheat, cover with a plate and leave to stand 1 hour.

3 Drain thoroughly then combine with rest of ingredients.

4 Work to an ultra-smooth mixture, bit by bit, in a food processor or strong blender. Otherwise finely mince. Leave aside, covered, temporarily.

How come a Middle Eastern style meat cake as far away as Louisiana? I've talked this through with historians and the most plausible explanation seems simple enough. Bulgar or kibbled wheat (also called cracked wheat) is a hangover from the Moorish influence on the Spanish and is still used for this one particular dish — I haven't found it in any other, except one. If some of you out there know more precise details, please write to me care of Absolute Press.

Kibby could be described as eccentric. A minced meat mix is used as a sandwich filling for a second meat mix, this time containing kibbled wheat which the locals have shortened to kibby. Dolloped with Creole sauce (page 62), it has the taste of success and I pass it on with pleasure but suggest you keep it for youthful get-togethers where quantity is perhaps more appreciated than quality. It's heavy going.

5 For filling, heat salad oil in a pan until sizzling.

6 Mix in onions, beef, salt and pine nuts. Cover and fry for 15 minutes. Remove from heat and cool slightly.

7 Spread half the mixture of meat and kibbled wheat over base of dish with a dampened hand. Cover with filling. Top with rest of first mixture, pressing it down well.

8 Smooth with your hand (dampened) and drizzle melted butter or margarine over the top. Score top into squares, or diamonds.

9 Bake 30 minutes in oven set to 180°C (350°F), Gas 4. Accompany with Creole sauce and a leafy salad.

Aubergine Casserole with Beef

SERVES 6

1kg (2lb) aubergines,
washed and dried
boiling salted water
25g (1oz) margarine
50g (2oz) onion, peeled
and chopped
50g (2oz) celery, scrubbed
and chopped
75g (3oz) washed green
pepper, de-seeded and
chopped
450g (1lb) lean minced
beef
¼ to ½ level tsp cayenne
pepper
1 to 2 level tsp salt
75g (3oz) fresh white
breadcrumbs
a little extra melted
margarine for trickling
over the top

1 Thinly peel aubergines
and cut flesh into cubes.
Cook in boiling water for
about 15 minutes or until
soft. Drain and finely mash.

2 Heat margarine in a pan.
Add onion, celery and pepper.
Fry gently until vegetables are
soft and transparent, keeping
pan covered.

3 Mix in beef and continue
to fry until dry and crumbly.
Stir in mashed aubergines,
pepper, salt and 50g (2oz)
breadcrumbs.

Made with one of Louisiana's most popular vegetables, this
easy-to-assemble casserole provides a first class main meal with
grilled or baked tomatoes.

4 Spread mixture into a 23
by 8cm (9 by 3 inch) greased
heatproof dish. Sprinkle
remaining crumbs on top,
moisten with the extra
margarine, reheat and brown
about 15 minutes in hot oven
set to 230°C (450°F) Gas 8.

Grillades and Grits

SERVES 8

*1kg (2lb) veal fillet or
turkey breast, thinly sliced
and beaten flat
4 tblsp salad oil
50g (2oz) plain flour
350g (12oz) onions, peeled
and finely chopped
225g (8oz) washed green
pepper, de-seeded and
finely chopped
175g (6oz) washed and
well-scrubbed celery, finely
chopped
450g (1lb) ripe and bright
red tomatoes, blanched
and chopped
2 level tblsp tomato purée
½ level tsp dried thyme
2 level tsp paprika
2 or 3 shakes Tabasco or
⅛ tsp cayenne pepper
1 to 2 level tsp salt
275ml (½pt) hot water*

Like sausages and mash or burgers and chips, grillades and grits go together like two peas in a pod. Grillades is a kind of meat and vegetable stew made with what New Orleans cook, Joe Cahn, calls the trinity; onions, green pepper and celery. Joe is head of the New Orleans School of Cooking which he founded in 1975 and is a master craftsman when it comes to Louisiana specialities.

The recipe for Grillades, however, is not one of his but culled from another source and adapted by me when I returned from New Orleans. It's still very good! It is classed as Bayou Breakfast food and served with hominy grits, a creamy white cereal which looks like coarse semolina and is made from corn with the husks removed. You can get it over here expensively from stores like Harrods but I have found North African couscous (also a cereal but made from wheat) a reasonable substitute and it's on sale at my local minimarket at a sensible price. Certainly you should find it in any ethnic food shop and, like the corn grits, it can be eaten for breakfast with milk. It makes an amicable change from porridge, but don't tell the Scots.

1 Wash and dry veal or turkey breast and cut into pieces measuring about 8 by 10cm (3 by 4 inches).

2 Sizzle oil in a large pan. Add veal or turkey and fry until meat turns from pink to white. Remove to a plate for the time being.

3 Add flour to oil in pan to make a roux. Fry over a lowish heat, stirring, until it turns gingersnap tan.

4 Mix in onions, pepper and celery. Cover pan and cook gently for 15 minutes, stirring occasionally.

5 Replace veal or turkey. Add tomatoes, purée, thyme, paprika, Tabasco or cayenne, salt and water.

6 Stir well to mix, cover and simmer gently for about 45 minutes. Move stew round occasionally. Serve with grits (page 83).

Veal Oscar

SERVES 6

**6 escalopes of veal (each 125g or 4oz), beaten until very thin and flat
seasoned plain flour for coating
125g (4oz) butter or margarine
2 tblsp salad oil
450g (1lb) crabmeat
Hollandaise sauce
(pages 65, 66, 67)
12 thick asparagus spears, freshly cooked**

A total indulgence for rich occasions and akin to the trendy Surf and Turf — fish and meat cooked together. Though featured on fashionable restaurant menus, recipes for it in books are hard to find and I am not exactly certain of the precise combination of ingredients. There again, it may be up to the individual.

1 Coat veal with flour and fry in 75g (3oz) butter or margarine to which the oil has been added. Allow about 2 to 3 minutes per side. Keep hot.

2 Heat rest of butter or margarine until sizzling. Mix in crabmeat and warm through for about 3 minutes, stirring.

3 Arrange escalopes on 6 hot dinner plates. Top each with crabmeat then coat with warm Hollandaise sauce. Garnish with asparagus.

Beef Daube

SERVES 10

2kg (4lb) piece of boned beef for roasting with minimal fat
40g (1½oz) margarine
450g (1lb) onions, peeled and finely chopped
175g (6oz) washed green pepper, de-seeded and finely chopped
2 garlic cloves, peeled and crushed
1½ level tblsp plain flour
3 slightly rounded tblsp tomato purée
¼ tsp Tabasco
2 to 3 level tsp salt
1 level tsp mixed herbs
575ml (1pt) boiling water
2 bay leaves
1 level tsp Cajun seasoning, optional (see page 118)

Very New Orleans, very French, very much a classy dish for high-powered entertaining. It is based on the classic Boeuf en Daube with the odd twist here and there.

1 Wash and dry beef.

2 Heat margarine until hot in large saucepan. Add beef and fry briskly on all sides until well-sealed and brown. Remove to a plate.

3 Add onions, pepper and garlic to remaining margarine and fry until light gold. Stir in flour and cook 2 to 3 minutes, stirring all the time.

4 Blend in purée, Tabasco, salt, herbs and the boiling water. Add bay leaves and seasoning if used. Replace beef, bring slowly to boil and at once reduce heat.

5 Simmer gently over minimal heat for 3 hours or until meat is tender.

6 Top up with a little boiling water every now and then if sauce seems to be thickening up too much. Serve carved into slices with the sauce. Accompany with rice.

Red Beans and Rice

SERVES 4

175g (6oz) streaky bacon, chopped
175g (6oz) onions, peeled and chopped
75g (3oz) celery, scrubbed and chopped
125g (4oz) washed green pepper, de-seeded and chopped
1 heaped tblsp finely chopped parsley
1 or 2 garlic cloves, peeled and crushed
¼ level tsp ground bay leaves
⅛ to ¼ tsp Tabasco
2 level tblsp tomato purée
1 can (425g or 15oz) red kidney beans, undrained
salt and pepper to taste

1 Fry bacon over lowish heat until the fat runs. Add prepared vegetables, cover pan and cook gently for 15 minutes to soften.

2 Stir in all remaining ingredients. Cover pan again and simmer for 30 minutes, stirring twice. Serve with freshly cooked rice.

In the old days, when housewives were busy attending to their Monday wash, time was short and fancy meals were the last thing in their heads. This resulted in the simple and traditional Red Beans and Rice, made because the water was on the boil anyway and why not take the opportunity of cooking the beans at the same time? Although the washing machine has taken over from the wash boiler, the beany brew keeps going strong; revised editions are tastier than the originals though have more vegetables and less carne. Not a bad thing.

Stuffed Peppers

SERVES 3

**6 small to medium sized
washed green peppers,
each 75g (3oz)
boiling water
50g (2oz) long grain rice
125ml (4 fluid oz) water
¼ level tsp salt
25g (1oz) margarine
150g (5oz) onions, peeled
and chopped
50g (2oz) celery, well-
washed and chopped
225g (8oz) cooked meat
(ham, chicken, beef, pork)
chopped
1 grade 1 egg, beaten**

To cook
**150ml (¼pt) tomato juice
150ml (¼pt) stock or water
½ to 1 level tsp salt**

*A different arrangement altogether for the filling, made princi-
pally with cooked ingredients, packed into the peppers and
oven-heated with a "gravy" of tomato juice.*

1 Cut tops off peppers and
discard, then remove seeds.
Put into a saucepan, cover
with boiling water and cook
5 to 7 minutes or until the
crispness goes. Drain
thoroughly.

2 Cook rice in the water
and salt for about 10 to 12
minutes or until light and
fluffy. Transfer to a mixing
bowl.

3 Sizzle margarine in a
saucepan. Add onions and
celery and fry gently for
about 5 to 7 minutes or until
soft. Add to rice with the
cooked meat and egg. Mix
thoroughly.

4 Pack into peppers and
place inside a smallish roasting tin. Mix together tomato
juice, stock or water and salt.
Spoon over peppers.

5 Bake, uncovered, for 35
to 40 minutes in oven set to
180°C (350°F), Gas 4.

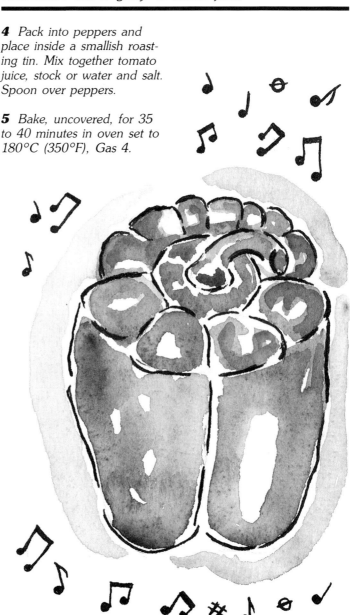

Boudin

SERVES 8 TO 10

350g (12oz) pig's liver, sliced
milk
450g (1lb) stewing pork, minced
175g (6oz) easy cook long grain rice
350ml (12 fluid oz) boiling water
2 level tsp salt
175g (6oz) onions, peeled and grated
5 tblsp boiling water
1 medium sized bunch of spring onions, chopped

1 Soak liver in milk to cover for 1 hour. Drain, rinse and simmer gently in boiling salted water to cover. Keep lid on pan and allow about 30 minutes. Drain.

2 Repeat with the pork, drain and reserve the water. Mince liver and pork together.

3 Put into bowl and leave aside temporarily. Cook rice in boiling water and salt for 15 minutes or until rice grains are plump and tender and have absorbed all the liquid. Add to liver and pork.

4 Stir in onions, reserved pork liquid, water and spring onions. Re-adjust seasoning to taste.

A Louisiana "fast food" sausage based on rice and pork. Or if not a sausage, then an accompaniment to roast meat and poultry. Or a cocktail snack — read on.

5 Transfer smoothly to a 30 by 25cm (12 by 8 inch) greased roasting tin. Leave uncovered then reheat and brown for 30 minutes in oven set to 225°C (425°F), Gas 7.

Boudin Sausages
Pack into sausage cases, size to suit, and reheat in hot water.

Boudin Bites
Roll Boudin mixture into small balls, coat with egg, toss in toasted breadcrumbs and deep fry until crisp and brown.

Chicken Fricassée (1)

SERVES 6 TO 8

**2kg (4lb) chicken joints
plain flour well seasoned
with salt and pepper
40g (1½oz) margarine or
white cooking fat
(vegetable)
75g (3oz) onion, peeled
and finely chopped
725ml (1¼pt) hot water or
chicken stock
1 bay leaf
½ level tsp mixed herbs
1 heaped tblsp chopped
parsley
extra salt and pepper to
taste**

1 Wash and dry chicken then coat in the seasoned flour.

2 Heat margarine or cooking fat in a large but fairly shallow pan (I use a frying pan with lid).

3 Mix in onion and fry fairly briskly until just beginning to turn pale gold.

4 Add chicken joints and fry until well browned on all sides, turning twice.

5 Pour in water or stock then add the bay leaf, herbs and parsley.

If you've ever had a British Chicken Fricassée (based on the French), in a sort of bland Bechamel sauce tasting of bay leaves and cloves, forget it. The Creole version is made of stronger stuff, even in its simplest form. Two recipes follow.

6 Bring slowly to the boil, reduce heat and cover. Simmer about 45 to 50 minutes until chicken is tender. Taste gravy halfway through and adjust seasoning.

7 Serve with freshly cooked rice.

45

Chicken Fricassée (2)

SERVES 6

2 tblsp oil
1½kg (3lb) chicken joints,
washed and well drained
2 level tblsp plain flour
125g (4oz) onions, peeled
and finely chopped
50g (2oz) well-scrubbed
celery, finely chopped
1 garlic clove, peeled and
crushed
225g (8oz) blanched
tomatoes, skinned and
chopped
3 level tblsp finely
chopped parsley
1 bouquet garni bag
450ml (¾pt) boiling water
2 pinches cayenne pepper
1 to 1½ level tsp salt

Here we're back to the old mix of roux, celery, onions, tomatoes and garlic. A sturdy approach and one which works out well – try it with Corn Bread (page 87) instead of rice for a change.

1 Heat oil in a pan until sizzling and really hot. Add chicken and fry until well-browned on all sides. Remove to a plate.

2 Add flour to oil in pan to form a roux. Cook slowly until gingersnap tan.

3 Mix in onions, celery and garlic. Fry about 7 minutes, stirring often.

4 Add tomatoes, parsley, bouquet garni bag and water. Slowly bring to boil, stirring continuously. Season with the pepper and salt.

5 Replace chicken, reduce heat and cover pan. Simmer about 45 to 50 minutes or until chicken is tender. Stir a few times to prevent sticking.

Louisiana Duck

SERVES 6

6 duck portions
50g (2oz) margarine or
bacon dripping
2 tsp salad oil
350g (12oz) onions, peeled
and chopped
125g (4oz) celery, well-
scrubbed and chopped
175g (6oz) washed green
pepper, de-seeded and
chopped
3 level tblsp plain flour
150ml (¼pt) warm chicken
stock or water
1 level tsp herbes de
Provence
1 can (400g or 14oz)
mushrooms and their
liquor
1 to 1½ level tsp salt
75ml (3 fluid oz) sweet
sherry

Flattered with sweet sherry and teased with herbs, you will warm to this classy duck dish using portions instead of a whole bird which are that much easier to negotiate. Better still, when you can find them, are boned duck breasts which are moist, tender, beautifully flavoured and unwasteful. To reduce greasiness, I remove all skin and fat before cooking.

1 *Skin duck then wash and dry with kitchen paper towels.*

2 *Heat margarine or dripping with oil in a pan until sizzling. Add duck and fry briskly on all sides until golden. Remove to a plate.*

3 *Add prepared vegetables to pan. Fry over medium heat until soft and pale gold.*

4 *Stir in flour to form a roux and cook until deep biscuity; 2 to 3 minutes.*

5 *Gradually blend in stock or water, then mix in herbs, mushrooms with liquor and salt. Bring to a slow boil, stirring.*

6 *Replace duck, cover and simmer 45 minutes. Stir in sherry. Serve with rice.*

Alligator Sauce Piquante

Sauce Piquante
2 tblsp salad oil
2 level tblsp plain flour
225g (8oz) onions, peeled
and finely chopped
175g (6oz) washed green
peppers, de-seeded and
chopped
50g (2oz) celery, well-
scrubbed and finely chopped
2 garlic cloves, peeled and
crushed
¼ to ½ tsp Tabasco
1 can (400g or 14oz)
sieved Italian tomatoes
450ml (¾pt) hot water or
homemade beef stock
1¼ level tsp salt
1 rounded tsp paprika
½ level tsp allspice
3 bay leaves
2 level tsp dark brown
soft sugar

Alligator
450g (1lb) packet of
dressed meat, labelled
marinated and tenderised
25g (1oz) concentrated
butter
275ml (about ½pt) water

Garnish
3 heaped tblsp chopped
parsley
2 level tblsp chopped
spring onions

Unquestionably, an acquired taste − not mine − and as highly esteemed in Louisiana as truffles are in France, alligator is a protected animal but some is hunted and flown into British markets direct from Louisiana. Again, I quote from my favourite little book, French Acadian cooking by Bobby Potts, and please do listen if you're an animal lover and let me off the hook.

"As we mentioned earlier, Cajuns eat everything − even alligator meat. Actually alligator meat is delicious. The tail meat is white and as sweet as crabmeat. Other parts are darker. Recently alligators have been so conscientiously protected that in some areas there is a problem of over population. A very limited and carefully controlled hunting season opens once a year, so occasionally a few people are afforded a taste of the meat. It will probably reach the markets in the near future. Coon, squirrel, possum and nutria also make tasty dishes. Although the natives refer to the animal as a "nutria rat" be-cause of his long tail, he is a very clean, vegetarian mammal who spends much time in the water feeding on tiny water plants. The meat, cooked in a rich tomato gravy is a gourmet treat. Duck, goose, all game birds and even poule d'eau (coot) go into gumbo and other wonderful concoctions."

Alligator is available from Billingsgate and has a sub-dued, unusual flavour somewhere between veal and chicken. Sauce Piquante is a classic for game and some alternatives for the ways you can use it follow:

1 Make the sauce first. For roux, heat oil in a saucepan, add flour and cook, stirring constantly, until it turns to colour of a gingersnap; about 2 minutes.

2 Mix in onions, peppers, celery and garlic. Fry 5 minutes until vegetables soften. Stir in all remaining ingredients.

3 Bring slowly to boil, stirring continuously. Cover and simmer over low heat for 45 minutes.

4 Prepare alligator. Wash and thoroughly dry then cut into cubes. Heat butter in a pan until hot then add alli-gator, a few pieces at a time. At this stage it shrivels up a bit. Fry until golden.

5 In order to soften, simmer in water to cover until it feels soft (keep pan covered) or pressure cook for 20 minutes at full.

6 Add, with liquid from pan, to the Sauce Piquante and simmer, covered, for a further 30 minutes.

7 Serve in bowls with freshly cooked rice in each, rather like Gumbo (page 16). Sprinkle each portion with parsley and onions.

French Style Fried Frog Legs

**2 frog legs per person
vinegar, to cover
1 onion, chopped
1 clove garlic, peeled and
crushed
batter, for coating (see
page 117)
deep fat, for frying
1 lemon, sliced or cut into
wedges**

1 Wash the frog legs thoroughly and dry on kitchen paper towels.

2 Marinate the frog legs for 3 hours in mild vinegar to which the onion and garlic have been added. Drain and dry.

3 Coat with batter or dip in beaten eggs and breadcrumbs. Deep fry until legs float to the top. Turn over and continue to fry until deep gold.

4 Drain and serve with lemon wedges or slices.

I quote from a wonderful book by Bobby Potts I brought back with me from Louisiana. It is called French Acadian Cooking in the Louisiana Bayou Country and describes this basic dish with great clarity and charm.

"Ouaouaron is the French word for bullfrog and the sound of it closely resembles his nightly ramblings in the swamp. Frog hunting at night with gigs and headlamps was always one of the greater pleasures of Cajun men. Well cooked tender frogs are fitting food for the Greek Gods, and one hears many Acadian names taken from Greek mythology, such as Achille, Ulysses, Telesphore and Theophile." One addition; the major area for the frog industry is in a place called Rayne, about 20 miles west of Lafayette.

The legs, incidentally, taste like chicken and should you come across them on your shopping expedition here or in France, this is what you should do:

Eggs

Eggs Sardou (1)

SERVES 4

**2 muffins, warmed through
in the oven
anchovy paste such as
Gentlemen's Relish
4 artichoke hearts, warmed
through in a dish over a
pan of boiling water
4 poached eggs, freshly
cooked
Hollandaise sauce
(page 65, 66, 67)**

1 Split muffins and put on
to 4 warm plates. Spread
thinly with the anchovy paste.

2 Top each muffin half with
an artichoke heart followed
by an egg.

3 Coat with Hollandaise
sauce. Serve straight away.

*A masterpiece of innovation, Eggs Sardou were created by
Antoine's restaurant in New Orleans in honour of the French
playwright, Victorien Sardou. No two recipes are now alike so
I have opted for a variation of the original with another to
follow.*

Eggs Sardou (2)

*Thaw a 225g (8oz) pack of
chopped spinach. Cook until
minimal water remains then
stir in 3 tablespoons double
cream and seasoning to taste.
Cover muffin halves with the
creamed spinach instead of
the anchovy paste.*

Eggs Benedict

**4 large slices of toast or 2 toasted muffin halves
4 slices of ham or 4 rashers back bacon, freshly fried or grilled
4 poached eggs, freshly cooked
Hollandaise sauce (page 65, 66, 67)
paprika**

No brunch, anywhere in North America, would be complete without Eggs Benedict, basically poached eggs on ham or bacon toast topped with Hollandaise sauce (page 65, 66, 67). Louisiana is no exception to what has become an unwritten brunch rule and the eggs are one of the specialities of the famous French New Orleans restaurant, Antoine's, and the Court of Two Sisters. My recipe is a variation of the two.

1 Stand toast or muffins on 4 warm plates and top with cold ham or bacon.

2 Top with poached eggs then coat with freshly made Hollandaise sauce. Sprinkle lightly with paprika for a hint of colour.

Consideration

The dish is rich enough as it is, which is why I have left the bread unbuttered or unmargarined, as the case may be.

French Omelet

SERVES 2

75g (3oz) streaky bacon,
chopped
50g (2oz) pickled red
pepper, drained and
chopped
50g (2oz) green pepper,
washed and chopped
50g (2oz) onion, peeled
and grated
75g (3oz) blanched and
chopped tomatoes
75g (3oz) cooked potatoes,
cut into small cubes

Omelet
4 grade 1 eggs
2 tblsp milk
2 tblsp water
½ to 1 level tsp salt,
depending on taste
15g (½oz) butter or
margarine for frying

1 Put bacon into a pan and cook gently until fat runs. Increase heat. Add next 4 ingredients and fry until vegetables soften and just begin to turn golden brown. Don't frizzle. Stir in potatoes.

2 Beat together eggs with milk and water. Season with salt.

3 Sizzle butter or margarine in a 20cm (8 inch) non-stick pan. Swirl round until base and sides are covered then heat until fat turns a light gold.

We know this better, perhaps, as the Spanish omelet but Acadians claim it as theirs so in Louisiana it's decidedly French. No doubts at all. Don't argue.

4 Pour in egg mixture and fry quickly, pushing edges to middle, until omelet has set and only the top is covered with a thinnish layer of moisture.

5 Cover one side with bacon mixture, fold in half and slide omelet out on to a plate. Cut into 2 portions and serve straight away.

53

Vegetables and Salads

Aubergines (Egg Plant) Parmigiani

SERVES 6

700g (1½lb) aubergines (choose smallish ones) boiling salted water

Crumb Mixture
125g (4oz) fresh breadcrumbs
50g (2oz) butter (concentrated for preference)

Cheese Mixture
175g (6oz) Cheddar cheese grated
25g (1oz) Parmesan cheese grated

Sauce
4 tblsp salad oil
225g (8oz) onions, peeled and chopped
2 garlic cloves, peeled and crushed
1 level tsp dried basil
1 level tsp dried oregano
4 tblsp sweet white wine (perfect is Muscat de Beaumes-de-Venise)
1 can (400g or 14oz) sieved Italian tomatoes
2 level tsp salt
2 rounded tblsp chopped parsley

Adopted from Italy, this deliciously tasty main course is what I call labour intensive although I have by-passed some of the tedious processes to make the whole thing more practical.

Knowing that people in Britain are not sold on Parmesan cheese if it's used in any quantity, I have included a small amount only and combined it with Cheddar. It's worked well.

1 Wash and dry aubergines. Cook, unpeeled and whole, in boiling salted water until tender. Drain, cool and gently squeeze dry. Cut into thickish slices.

2 For crumb mixture, fry breadcrumbs in the butter until golden. Leave aside for the moment.

3 Combine both cheeses.

4 To make sauce, sizzle oil in a pan. Add onions and garlic and fry until pale gold. Mix in all remaining ingredients. Simmer 7 minutes, stirring.

5 To complete, fill a 1.75 litre (3pt) greased dish with alternate layers of sauce, aubergines, crumbs and cheese. Begin with sauce and end with cheese.

6 Reheat and brown 30 minutes in oven set to 190°C (375°F) Gas 5.

55

Louisiana Aubergine Barges

SERVES 4

**2 large aubergines (1kg
or 2lb)
boiling salted water
3 tblsp oil
125g (4oz) onions, peeled
and finely chopped
125g (4oz) well-scrubbed
celery, finely chopped
125g (4oz) washed green
pepper, de-seeded and
chopped
75g (3oz) button
mushrooms, trimmed and
chopped
1 garlic clove, peeled and
crushed
50g (2oz) fresh
breadcrumbs
2 level tblsp tomato purée
75g (3oz) pecan nuts,
chopped
125g (4oz) Cheddar
cheese, grated
1 level tsp salt
25g (1oz) butter or
margarine, melted**

Shining, purple aubergines (called eggplants down South) are one of the most popular vegetables in Louisiana and this is my adaptation of several recipes, combined to produce a main course with enough zip to satisfy even the most jaded vegetarian palate.

1 *Wash aubergines and wipe dry. To make barges, halve aubergines and cut out centres. The hollowed out aubergine halves should be 1cm or ½ inch thick.*

2 *Chop aubergine centres and leave aside for the moment. Cook aubergine halves in boiling salted water for 5 minutes. Drain and cool.*

3 *Heat oil in a pan. Add onions and chopped aubergine then sizzle until light gold.*

4 *Mix in celery and pepper. Fry 5 minutes. Add mushrooms and garlic. Fry, uncovered, over a medium heat for 15 minutes.*

5 *Stir in crumbs, purée, three-quarters of the nuts, half the cheese and the salt.*

6 *Mound into aubergine halves, sprinkle with rest of nuts and cheese then trickle butter or margarine over the top. Heat and brown for 20 minutes in oven set to 200°C (400°F), Gas 6. Serve with Congealed Tomato Salad (page 60).*

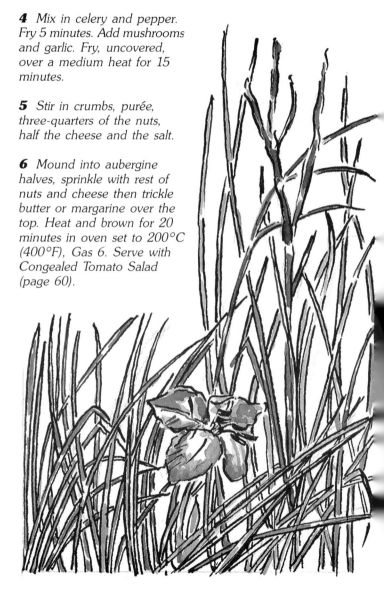

Mirliton Pirogues

4 mirlitons
boiling salted water
50g (2oz) butter or
margarine
175g (6oz) onions, peeled
and grated
125g (4oz) fresh white
breadcrumbs
1 grade 1 or 2 egg, beaten
1 level tsp salt
⅛ tsp cayenne pepper
(optional)
400g (14oz) frozen and
defrosted prawns

How can I describe mirlitons to you? They are mildly flavoured, a member of the squash family − like pumpkin and marrow − and the shape of a large pear (they are called the vegetable pear in the deep South). Each has four to five elongated ridges on its body and the colour is reminiscent of a Granny Smith apple or, for those who remember bygone days, that beautiful 1930's apple green used by everyone for counterpanes and cushions.

Mirlitons grow in profusion whenever the sun scalds and are an abundant crop in the cotton growing states of the US; South Carolina, Louisiana and Georgia. We import them under the better known names of chayote or christophene and they can be found, certainly in London and South East England, in leading supermarket chains and ethnic food shops.

A pirogue, by the way, is a type of canoe used in the bayous for transport and fishing in the southern part of Louisiana. Vegetables which are halved and filled resemble canoes in shape and are therefore referred to as pirogues.

1 Wash and dry mirlitons and cook in boiling salted water until tender. Cover but leave lid ajar to prevent boiling over.

2 Allow about 45 minutes cooking time and check periodically for tenderness by pushing a wooden cocktail stick into the mirlitons. If it slides in graciously, you can take it they are ready.

3 Drain and cool. Halve lengthwise and gently remove seeds which look like flat butter beans, extra large. In Louisiana, they are sometimes added to salads.

4 Carefully scoop flesh out of mirliton halves, taking care not to break through the delicate skins. Chop up flesh coarsely.

5 Sizzle butter or margarine in a pan. Add onions and cook, covered, for about 5 to 7 minutes until soft but still pale.

6 Mix in chopped mirlitons and cook over medium heat until minimal liquid remains. Leave uncovered, stir occasionally.

7 Mix in rest of ingredients and pile into pirogues. Transfer to an oiled baking tray and reheat for 15 minutes in oven set to 220°C (425°F), Gas 7. Eat with freshly boiled rice.

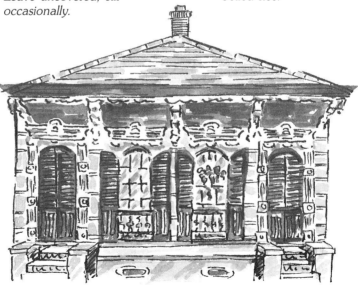

Mirliton Salad

2 mirlitons
boiling salted water
4 tblsp French dressing
4 large lettuce leaves,
washed and dried
3 spring onions, trimmed
and washed
125g (4oz) cream cheese,
at kitchen temperature
2 to 3 tblsp single cream
salt and pepper to taste
about 1½ level tblsp
washed and chopped
parsley

A cool approach for summer with enough scope for personal imagination. You'll see in a minute.

Alternatives

1 Cut each mirliton half lengthwise into slices. Arrange on lettuce lined plates with sliced tomatoes. Coat lightly with extra dressing.

2 Toss fresh or defrosted frozen prawns in Remoulade dressing (page 63/64). Mound on top of mirliton halves. Stand on lettuce-lined plates.

3 Fill mirliton halves with potato salad (page 78). Stand on lettuce-lined plates.

1 Peel and halve mirlitons then remove large seeds. Cook the halves in boiling salted water until tender, allowing 35 to 45 minutes. Keep pan two-thirds covered.

2 Drain mirlitons, return to pan and coat with dressing. Cover and leave until completely cold.

3 Arrange lettuce leaves on 4 bread and butter plates then top each with half a mirliton, cut sides uppermost.

4 Chop spring onions. Beat cream cheese and cream together until light. Stir in onions then season to taste with salt and pepper.

5 Pile mixture on top of mirlitons, placing it in centre of each. Sprinkle with parsley and serve at room temperature.

Okra Salad

SERVES 4

**450g (1lb) small sized okra
boiling salted water
50g (2oz) onion, peeled
and grated
3 to 4 tblsp French
dressing**

This exotic vegetable finds its way into many Louisiana dishes, even salad. Serve it "re-al cool" with meat, chicken, duck and fried fish. Or keep it as a starter for guests with curiosity.

1 Wash okra then top and tail. Cook in boiling salted water until just tender – don't overcook.

2 Drain – toss with onion and French dressing. Cover, leave until cool then well chill in the refrigerator before serving.

Congealed Tomato Salad

MAKES 8 LITTLE JELLIES

2 sachets powdered gelatine
150ml (¼pt) cold water
575ml (1pt) tomato juice
350g (12oz) ripe tomatoes, blanched and skinned
75g (3oz) onion, peeled and cut into chunky pieces
1 garlic clove, peeled and halved
50g (2oz) washed green pepper, de-seeded and cut into pieces
3 or 4 drops Tabasco
1 to 1½ level tsp salt

1 Tip gelatine into a saucepan. Stir in water and leave to soak and soften for 5 minutes.

2 Transfer to a low heat and stir gently until completely dissolved. Leave aside for the time being.

3 Put remaining ingredients into a blender goblet and run machine until mixture is completely smooth.

4 Pour gradually into the pan of dissolved gelatine and mix thoroughly. Transfer to 8 individual jelly moulds rinsed with cold water or use baby basins instead.

5 Refrigerate until set. Turn out onto lettuce-lined plates to serve.

Cool, refreshing and tangy, this jellied salad goes particularly well with jambalaya, or you can serve it as a summer starter atop leafy green lettuce leaves enhanced with French dressing.

Consideration
Instead of the fiddle of 8 moulds or basins, set mixture in one mould. Turn out and spoon portions on to plates.

60

Sauces and Preserves

Creole Sauce

SERVES 6

2 tblsp oil
125g (4oz) onion, peeled
and finely chopped
75g (3oz) celery, well-
scrubbed and finely
chopped
1 garlic clove, peeled and
crushed
125g (4oz) washed green
pepper, de-seeded and
finely chopped
1 can (400g or 14oz)
tomatoes
1 level tsp molasses or
molasses sugar
1 tblsp fresh lemon juice
⅛ tsp ground bay leaves
1 level tsp salt
Tabasco sauce

1 Sizzle oil in a pan. Add
next 4 ingredients and cook
over a moderate heat for
about 7 to 10 minutes or
until soft and only just beginning to turn golden.

2 Add tomatoes, crushing
each one against sides of
pan.

3 Stir in remaining ingredients,
bring slowly to boil and
simmer gently, with lid on
pan, for 15 minutes.

4 Stir 2 or 3 times and
serve as suggested.

Hot, hotter, hottest sums up this gutsy sauce which the locals
serve as a matter of course with meat loaves, sausages,
chicken, game, rice and pasta − even fried fish sometimes.
It can easily set you afire, which is why the quantity of
Tabasco has been left blank; it's up to you to add as much or
as little as you like. Note the sauce is unthickened with flour or
cornflour, relying on the vegetables to do the job instead.

Remoulade Sauce (1)

**MAKES JUST OVER
450ml (¾pt)**

**225g (8oz) mayonnaise
3 tblsp salad oil
2 to 3 level tsp powder
mustard
2 level tblsp trimmed
spring onions, washed and
chopped
1 level tblsp well-washed
and scrubbed celery,
chopped
1 rounded tblsp finely
chopped parsley
1 level tblsp creamed
horseradish sauce
1 level tsp dried tarragon
(optional)
1 level tblsp tomato purée
¼ level tsp cayenne pepper
3 level tsp paprika
1 tsp Worcester sauce
salt and pepper to taste**

Designed especially for seafood, this is a well-loved Louisiana sauce, based on the French classic recipe for Remoulade but with more ingredients and no anchovy. It is a warm-hearted blend of flavours, lively and characterful, on the hot side, bliss with lobster or chunky crabmeat. Or even monkfish that has been fried.

1 *Put mayonnaise and oil into a bowl and beat well together until smooth.*

2 *Gradually work in rest of ingredients.*

3 *Transfer to a lidded container and store in the refrigerator until needed.*

Remoulade Sauce (2)

**MAKES ABOUT
275ml (½pt)**

4 tblsp salad oil
2 tblsp red wine vinegar
2 level tblsp Creole
mustard
2 level tsp creamed
horseradish sauce
⅛ tsp Tabasco
1 level tsp paprika
75g (3oz) well-washed and
scrubbed celery, chopped
3 trimmed spring onions,
washed and chopped
2 level tblsp finely
chopped parsley

1 Beat all ingredients well together.

2 Transfer to a lidded container and store in the refrigerator until needed.

This is more in the style of a French dressing and contains Creole mustard (page 71). It is also used for seafood and is a classic for prawn or crab cocktails.

Hollandaise Sauce

ENOUGH FOR 6 SERVINGS

*125g (4oz) concentrated
butter
3 yolks from grade 2 eggs
3 tblsp boiling water
1 tblsp strained lemon
juice
1 tblsp white wine vinegar
pinch caster sugar
salt and white pepper to
taste*

The golden princess of all sauces, Hollandaise is a shining example (literally) of one of the world's greats, much admired by international gourmets, gourmands and chefs. It is a sauce we serve over here with salmon, salmon trout, sole, turbot, broccoli, artichoke hearts and asparagus. In the USA, it is a natural with Eggs Sardou and Eggs Benedict (pages 51/52), both brunch specials on high days and holidays. Hollandaise is rich, calorie-laden and always served warm.

1 Melt butter slowly in a saucepan and leave on one side temporarily until luke-warm.

2 Meanwhile, put yolks into the top of a double saucepan with simmering water underneath. Alternatively, use a small basin resting over a pan of simmering water.

3 Add 1 tblsp boiling water and whisk until yolks become bubbly and begin to thicken. Beat in second tablespoon of boiling water. Cook a few minutes more. Finally beat in last tablespoon of water.

4 Separately, heat lemon juice and vinegar until luke-warm. Beat into egg yolks and water.

5 As though you were making mayonnaise, beat in the melted butter teaspoon by teaspoon, whisking continuously.

6 When half the butter has been added and the sauce thickens and takes on a fluffy appearance, beat in remaining butter in a continuous stream. Add sugar, season to taste and serve straight away.

Consideration

1 If too thin, increase heat under the pan of water in order to cook the yolks a little bit more and thicken the sauce.

2 If too thick, beat in 1 or 2 tablespoons extra hot water.

3 If sauce curdles (heat too high and water became too hot in the pan), add an ice cube and stir round and round until sauce is smooth.

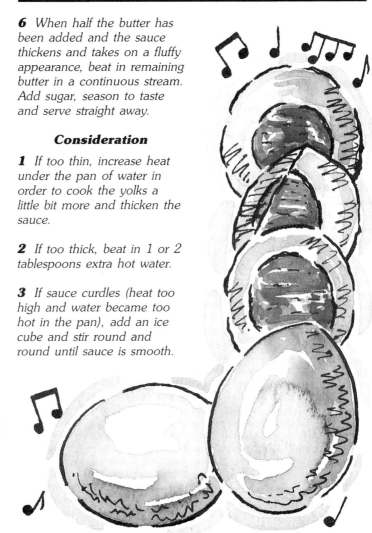

Hollandaise in the Blender

SERVES 4 TO 6

150g (5oz) concentrated butter
1 tblsp white wine vinegar
1 tblsp strained lemon juice
3 yolks from grade 2 eggs
¼ level tsp caster sugar
½ level tsp salt
white pepper to taste

1 Melt butter slowly in a pan then heat until hot but not starting to turn brown. Leave aside.

2 Separately, bring vinegar and lemon juice to the boil.

3 Put yolks into blender goblet with sugar, salt and the hot vinegar and lemon juice.

4 Cover and blend for 6 seconds. Remove lid and with blender set to maximum speed, add the hot butter in a steady slow stream.

5 The sauce will thicken beautifully and be ready in 45 seconds. Season with pepper and serve straight away.

A miracle of speed, this is a super sauce which takes a few minutes to prepare and no problems with curdling, overcooking, undercooking ...

Hollandaise in the Microwave

SERVES 4 TO 6

**125g (4oz) any slightly salted butter
1 tblsp strained lemon juice
2 yolks from grade 2 eggs
salt and pepper to taste
2 pinches of caster sugar**

So few people believe me when I tell them Hollandaise can be made in the microwave that I've given up preaching. But please have faith and your efforts will be rewarded.

1 Cut butter into cubes and put into a 275ml (½pt) glass Pyrex jug.

2 Leave uncovered and melt at full power for 1 to 1½ minutes or until butter is hot and foamy.

3 Whisk in lemon juice and yolks. Leave uncovered, return to the microwave and cook 30 seconds at full power.

4 Remove from oven and whisk. If Hollandaise looks on the thinnish side instead of being thickish and custardy, cook for a further 15 or 20 seconds, whisking once after 8 seconds.

5 Season to taste with salt, pepper and sugar and serve straight way.

Cocktail Sauce for Seafood (1)

**MAKES ABOUT
150ml (¼pt)**

**2 level tblsp chilli sauce
4 level tblsp tomato
ketchup
4 tblsp French dressing
strained juice of 2 large
lemons
25g (1oz) celery, well-
scrubbed and chopped
2 heaped tblsp chopped
chives or spring onions
1 level tblsp horseradish
sauce or creamed
horseradish
shake or two of Worcester
sauce
salt to taste**

With so much seafood to pick and choose from, the cocktail sauce is essential in Louisiana. But this one is on the very hot side and bites. You may therefore prefer to go for version two which is a milder affair altogether and more familiar to mortals over here who are not used to flame swallowing.

1 *Beat all ingredients well together with a fork or small whisk.*

2 *Toss with seafood or spoon over the top.*

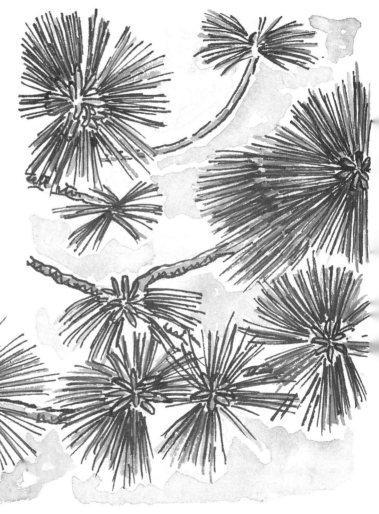

Cocktail Sauce for Seafood (2)

275ml (½pt) mayonnaise
2 level tblsp tomato purée
1 level tblsp creamed
horseradish sauce
1 level tblsp tomato
ketchup
2 tsp Worcester sauce
⅛ to ¼ tsp Tabasco
3 tsp strained lemon juice

A mayonnaise-based sauce, this one is classically French and the one most used in Europe for fish cocktails.

1 Mix all ingredients well together and use as required.

Mushroom Sauce

SERVES 6

25g (1oz) butter or margarine
50g (2oz) onion, peeled and finely chopped
175g (6oz) button mushrooms, trimmed and sliced
25g (1oz) plain flour
275ml (½pt) single cream
150ml (¼pt) chicken stock
½ level tsp French mustard
½ to 1 level tsp salt

Mild by Louisiana standards, this is a pleasant enough "spoon-over" effort for meat loaves, chicken and fish such as Mahi-Mahi (if you can ever find it).

1 Heat butter or margarine in a pan until it just begins to turn pale gold. Add onions and fry gently for 5 minutes.

2 Stir in mushrooms, simmer for 2 minutes then work in flour. Cook a further 2 minutes.

3 Gradually add cream and stock. Cook, stirring all the time, until sauce comes to the boil and thickens.

4 Simmer gently for 3 minutes. Add mustard and season with salt.

Cajun Mustard

**MAKES JUST OVER
150ml (¼pt)**

**50g (2oz) powder mustard
75g (3oz) caster sugar
50ml (2 fluid oz) wine
vinegar
50ml (2 fluid oz) corn oil
2 shakes Tabasco**

1 Beat all ingredients together until smoothly mixed.

2 Transfer to a screw-topped jar and store in the refrigerator.

3 Give the sauce a few days to mature before using. Stir round. Use as required.

Creole Mustard

This is seasoned mustard with grains, readily available over here usually in jars. It is slightly tangy and sharpened with vinegar.

A similar type of sauce is always served in Sweden with Gravlax (salmon preserved with dill, salt, sugar and pepper) and one wonders if the connection is coincidence or historical. It is an off-beat condiment, hot and sweet at the same time and mostly used to give a bit of kick to sauces and dressings. You'll either like it or you won't − it's an acquired taste.

Whisky Sauce (1)

SERVES 12

3 level tblsp cornflour
450ml (¾pt) cold water
225g (8oz) caster sugar
25g (1oz) butter or
margarine
3 egg yolks
6 to 8 tblsp whisky

1 Mix cornflour smoothly
with some of the cold water.
Add remainder and pour into
a saucepan.

2 Add sugar and butter or
margarine. Cook, stirring
constantly, until sauce comes
to the boil and thickens.
Simmer 2 minutes.

3 Remove from heat and
beat in egg yolks and whisky.
Serve with portions of pudding.

The classic sauce for Louisiana bread pudding, distinctively cheered with Bourbon. In the absence of American whisky, use Scottish or Irish. Rum instead if you prefer the taste.

Whisky Sauce (2)

SERVES 12

125g (4oz) butter
175g (6oz) icing sugar, sifted
1 egg yolk
125ml (4 fluid oz) whisky

An adaptation of a recipe from Joe Cahn, head of the New Orleans School of Cooking.

1 Melt butter in a saucepan. Mix in icing sugar and stir briskly over a moderate heat until mixture has thickened and all the butter is absorbed.

2 Remove from heat, add whisky, cool slightly and beat in the yolk.

3 Strain into a bowl and serve warm with bread pudding.

Consideration

Leave sauce until cold then whip until pale and slightly thickened. Serve with the hot bread pudding.

French Dressing

MAKES 150ml (¼pt)

5 tblsp oil (olive has the most flavour but peanut, grapeseed or corn are fine)
1 level tsp French mustard
¼ level tsp salt (more if preferred)
1 shake Tabasco sauce
2 shakes Worcester sauce
2 pinches of sugar
3 tblsp strained lemon juice or white wine vinegar (or a mixture of the two)

1 Pour oil into a basin and mix in next 5 ingredients.

2 Gradually beat in lemon juice or vinegar or a combination of the two. By now the dressing should hold together like an emulsion.

3 Use straight away as required.

Here we do have a problem because French dressing as we know it is called Vinaigrette in Louisiana though basically it's the same.

Fanciful offspring appear in books from time to time which seem far removed from the original but they are lively, tasty and full of bits to add a lilt to any salad. One such child is at the end.

Consideration

To make in quantity, quadruple all the ingredients and store in a screw-topped jar or bottle with cork. Shake well before using.

Vinaigrette Dressing Dressed Up

MAKES ABOUT 150ml (¼pt)
An Acadian number, designed for any kind of salad you can think of.

Make the basic French Dressing above then add 6 trimmed and finely chopped spring onions, 1 chopped hard boiled egg, 1 well-scrubbed and finely chopped celery stalk, 2 rounded tablespoons chutney, 1 rounded tablespoon finely chopped pickled red peppers, 1 tablespoon chopped chives and the same of parsley.

Red Pepper Jelly

SEVERAL JARS

350g (12oz) red peppers, washed and de-seeded
3 green chillies, washed and dried
350ml (12 fluid oz) cider or wine vinegar
1½kg (3lb) caster sugar
1 level tblsp salt
1 bottle (227ml or 8 fluid oz) Certo
red food colouring (optional)

A Southern oddity which I tried in Louisiana with a certain amount of trepidation. It was red, jellied, sweet, very peppery, totally unique and I expected it to taste like solidified cough linctus forced down me as a child for bronchitis. Actually it was surprisingly pleasant and went down a treat with fried catfish and Gumbo (pages 31 and 16). So, being me and loving a challenge, I came home and made it. What I didn't think of at the time was the amount of jelly the ingredients would yield so I am unable to tell you how many jars to have ready. Just more than you think which isn't much help. I'm sorry.

1 Cut red peppers into pieces. Slit open chillies, remove seeds and at once wash your hands to avoid burning the skin if you touch your lips, eyes, nose and so on.

2 Work peppers and chillies to a smooth purée in blender goblet or food processor. Scrape into a saucepan.

3 Add next 3 ingredients. Bring slowly to boil, stirring constantly until sugar dissolves. Simmer 5 minutes.

4 Stir in Certo and a few drops of colouring. Leave to stand 10 minutes then transfer to warm, dry jars. Cover when cold as you would jam. Store in dark cupboard.

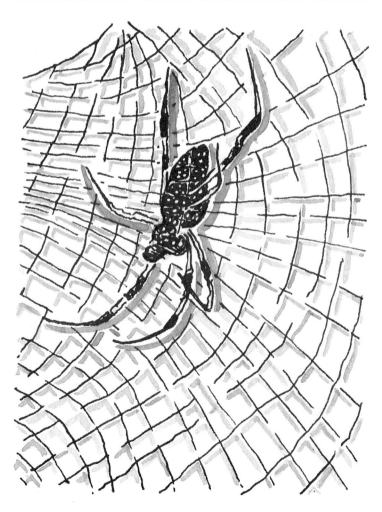

Bread and Butter Pickles

MAKES 2 JARS (each about 450g or 1lb)

1 large cucumber (unpeeled) washed and THINLY sliced
225g (8oz) onions, peeled and very thinly sliced
175ml (6 fluid oz) colourless distilled malt vinegar
175g (6oz) caster sugar
1 rounded tsp mixed pickling spice
2 level tsp salt
¼ level tsp mustard powder
¼ level tsp turmeric

1 Leave cucumber slices and onions to drain in a colander while preparing the liquid.

2 Pour vinegar and sugar into a saucepan. Slowly bring to boil, stirring all the time.

3 Mix in rest of ingredients then place cucumber and onions in the pan. Boil 2 minutes. Cool to lukewarm, transfer to jars and cover when cold. Store in the refrigerator.

If you're a pickles with everything buff, you'll know all about those appetising-looking pickled cucumbers in supermarkets and delis, greeny-gold, moderately-priced and obviously prepared with love and dedication by zealous picklers from a wide spread of European countries including Britain, Germany, Poland and Czechoslovakia. Why, I asked myself, do they always look nice, smell nice and taste nice − much better than my own efforts. Then I discovered the secret when I was knee-deep in cucumbers and surrounded by Southern cook books. Firstly a soupcon of turmeric turns the liquid into a warm gold and the combination of white sugar and white vinegar renders the pickles crisp and piquantly sweet-sour. What a triumph!

Originally, in the old days, the B and B's were always put into sandwiches to give the fillings added bite and flavour. Now they go with everything imaginable − burgers, steaks, fried fish, hot dogs; you name it.

Side Dishes

Acadian Potato Salad

SERVES 6 TO 8

**700g (1½lb) potatoes,
washed and peeled
boiling salted water
4 grade 1 or 2 hardboiled
eggs, shelled
125g (4oz) washed green
pepper, de-seeded and
chopped
75g (3oz) onion, peeled
and grated
125g (4oz) chopped-up
mustard pickle
225g (8oz) mayonnaise
1 level tsp French mustard
1 level tsp salt
pepper to taste
stuffed olives for decoration**

A very different kettle of fish from the tacky, salad-creamy mix we know and occasionally love or hate, Acadian potato salad is a one-off, luscious, golden and still considered by Louisiana purists to be THE partner for Chicken Gumbo. Give it a try, making sure it is well-chilled first so that you have a 'chaud-froid' with the hot gumbo. Quite a palate startler.

1 Cook potatoes in boiling salted water until soft but not falling to pieces. Drain, cool, completely then cut up into small dice. Transfer to a mixing bowl.

2 Chop or coarsely grate the eggs. Add to the potatoes with pepper, onion and mustard pickle.

3 Using a spoon, toss gently with the mayonnaise, mustard and salt. Season with pepper.

4 Transfer to a bowl and garnish with olives, sliced or left whole. Cover and refrigerate at least 2 hours before serving.

Rice Salad

SERVES 6 TO 8

A sort of all-purpose salad, eaten with anything from alligator to roast poultry.

Make exactly as the Acadian Potato Salad, using 450g (1lb) boiled rice instead of the potatoes.

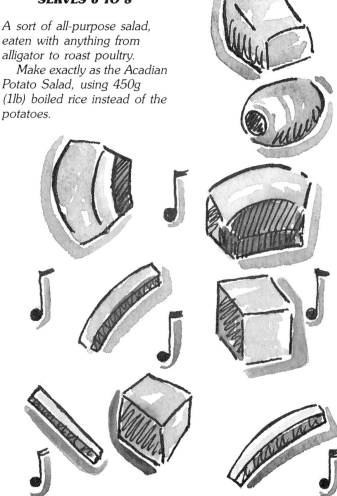

Mrs Smith's Broccoli Rice

SERVES 6 TO 8

**175g (6oz) easy-cook long
grain rice
350ml (12 fluid oz) boiling
water
1 level tsp salt
450g (1lb) fresh broccoli,
washed and shaken dry
extra boiling water
50g (2oz) butter or
margarine
125g (4oz) onion, peeled
and chopped
1 can condensed cream of
mushroom soup
200g (7oz) pack Cheddar
cheese spread
3 tblsp milk**

1 Tip rice into a pan with water and salt. Bring to boil, stirring. Cover and simmer 15 minutes. Fluff up with a fork. Leave aside temporarily.

2 Meanwhile, cut broccoli into thin slivers and par-boil in boiling water for 7 minutes. Drain.

3 Heat butter or margarine until sizzling. Add onion and fry over a moderate heat for about 5 minutes until soft but not brown.

4 Add broccoli and fry another 5 minutes with the onions.

5 Make a bed of rice in a shallow, heatproof dish. Arrange the broccoli on top of the rice.

Our first stop in Louisiana was at the Smith family's gazebo, a typical Mississippi holiday home overlooking a Bayou. It was constructed of wood, on two levels, complete with rocking chairs, rustic tableware on a vast table, fans whirring overhead and gargantuan amounts of Dr Pepper to quench the thirst of the world, housed in a double-fronted glass cabinet laden with ice. Magic.

After Houston, clammy, unbearably hot and deeply over-cast, this evening was like a breath of Brighton or Hastings in Summer, silver stars shimmering in an immaculately clear sky, the atmosphere friendly, unhurried, cheerful and refreshingly informal. And for all of us from England, our first taste of catfish and Hush Puppies, Jambalaya and Gumbo.

Before the meal, sipping Californian wine, cola and the by now familiar Doc Pepper, a slim and well-groomed lady, our hostess, approached.

"Your name is?" she asked.
"Sonia Allison", I replied, "and what should I call you?"
"Happy", she said.
"Yes, I can see that but what is your name?"
"I'm Happy", she insisted, looking at me oddly.
Her husband overheard the conversation and came across.
"This is ma wife. She's a happy wom'n so we calls her Happy!" He laughed, I crawled.

We became friends after that and towards the end of the evening, Happy came forward with two of her best recipes written on cards headed "From the recipe file of Happy Smith". These are for you.

Broccoli rice is a handsome accompaniment for shellfish, fried fish, freshly grilled gammon steaks and roast chicken. Or you can treat it as a vegetarian main course with a mixed salad beside.

6 Gently heat together the mushroom soup, cheese and milk. Spoon this mixture over the broccoli rice.

7 Reheat in the oven for 20 minutes at 220°C (425°F), Gas 7.

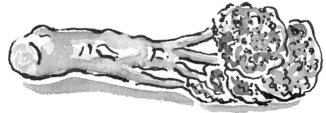

Spanish Rice

A glory hallelujah with roasts of chicken and duck.

225g (8oz) easy-cook long grain rice
275ml (½pt) boiling water
1 level tsp salt
2 tblsp salad oil
175g (6oz) onions, peeled and finely chopped
125g (4oz) washed green pepper, de-seeded and chopped
1 can (400g or 14oz) peeled tomatoes
1 level tsp Cajun seasoning, optional (see page 118)
1 level tsp salt

1 Cook rice as in previous recipe with water and salt.

2 Heat oil in a pan. Add onions and peppers. Fry fairly gently for a few minutes until soft but still pale in colour.

3 Add tomatoes and crush down against sides of pan with a fork or spoon.

4 Mix in rice and Cajun seasoning (if used) with the salt.

5 Transfer to a greased 1.2 litre (2pt) dish and bake 20 to 25 minutes in oven set to 190°C (375°F), Gas 5.

Dirty Rice

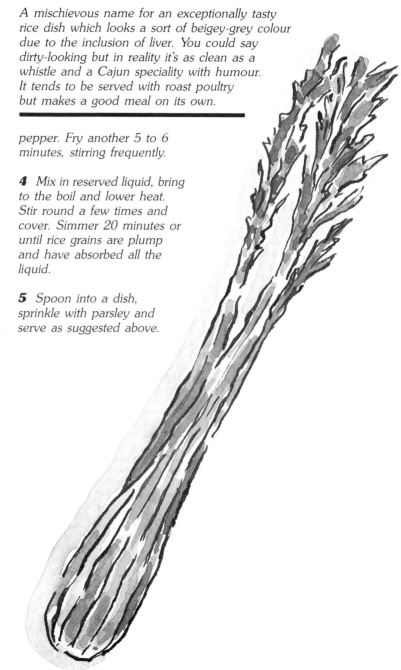

SERVES 4–6

175g (6oz) duck, chicken or turkey livers
cold water and hot water
25g (1oz) vegetable fat or margarine
1 garlic clove, peeled and crushed
50g (2oz) onion, peeled and chopped
6 spring onions, trimmed and chopped
50g (2oz) celery, scrubbed and very thinly sliced
75g (3oz) washed green pepper, de-seeded and chopped
225g (8oz) lean minced beef (in Louisiana it would be poultry giblets)
225g (8oz) easy-cook long grain rice
2 level tsp salt
¼ level tsp cayenne pepper
2 slightly rounded tblsp chopped parsley

A mischievous name for an exceptionally tasty rice dish which looks a sort of beigey-grey colour due to the inclusion of liver. You could say dirty-looking but in reality it's as clean as a whistle and a Cajun speciality with humour. It tends to be served with roast poultry but makes a good meal on its own.

1 Wash livers and put into a saucepan with cold water to cover. Bring to boil, lower heat and cover. Simmer about 20 minutes. Remove livers and mince or finely chop.

2 Drain liver stock into a measuring jug and make up to 575ml (1pt) with hot water. Leave aside for the moment.

3 Heat fat or margarine in a pan, add garlic and vegetables then fry 5 minutes over medium heat. Stir in beef, liver, rice, salt and cayenne pepper. Fry another 5 to 6 minutes, stirring frequently.

4 Mix in reserved liquid, bring to the boil and lower heat. Stir round a few times and cover. Simmer 20 minutes or until rice grains are plump and have absorbed all the liquid.

5 Spoon into a dish, sprinkle with parsley and serve as suggested above.

Green Beans in Brown Sauce

SERVES 3 TO 4

**450g (1lb) bobby,
runners sliced on the
diagonal, or topped and
tailed French beans
1 level tsp salt
boiling water to cover
2 tblsp salad or olive oil
2 level tblsp plain flour
50g (2oz) onion, peeled
and grated
275ml (½pt) bean water**

1 Wash beans and cut the
bobby ones or French into
half or thirds depending on
size. The runners you will
have already cut.

2 Put into a pan with salt
and water. Bring to boil, reduce heat and cover. Cook
until tender, about 10 minutes.

3 Meanwhile, heat oil in a
pan until sizzling. Stir in flour
to form a roux and cook
until light brown. Allow about
3 minutes and stir constantly.

4 Add onion and fry 5
minutes, again stirring.

5 Drain beans and reserve
275ml (½pt) of the water.
Gradually stir it into the roux
and onion mixture. Cook,
stirring, until sauce comes to
the boil and thickens.

6 Replace beans, heat
through and serve with meat,
poultry or fish.

We are not a bean family. I enjoy them occasionally on toast
or with sausages and mash. Simon, my son, puts up with
them (the red kidneys) in a Chilli but they play havoc with his
digestive system and embarrassment keeps him indoors for
several hours afterwards. My husband, a mild and gentle man,
views beans, all beans, with the same kind of disdain he keeps
in reserve for disco music in shops, people who kick cats,
cruelty to children, those who drop litter in public places and
the ice cream man, with van, who disturbs our doze every
Sunday afternoon during the summer months with the
fractured strains of Greensleeves.

When I threatened him with these Acadian green beans,
he agreed to eat them, no, try them, on condition he could
have a double helping of pudding. And they are so good, too.

Grits

575ml (1pt) milk, water or a mixture of milk and water
165g (5½oz) hominy grits or 175g (6oz) cous-cous
15g (½oz) butter or margarine
1 to 1½ level tsp salt

1 Pour liquid into a pan. Add grits or cous-cous. Bring to boil, stirring constantly.

2 Add last two ingredients. Two-thirds cover and cook over minimal heat for 15 minutes.

Consideration

If preferred, use meat or poultry stock instead of milk and/or water.

A full description of hominy grits is with the Grillade recipe on page 39. Now all that's left is the cooking.

Hush Puppies

MAKES 15 to 16

225g (8oz) cornmeal (polenta)
1 rounded tblsp plain flour
50g (2oz) onion, peeled and grated
1 level tsp salt
1 or 2 grindings of black pepper
1½ level tsp baking powder
275ml (½pt) boiling water
1 grade 2 egg, beaten
deep oil for frying

These are fried cornmeal fritters, generally served with fried fish. They are marvellously flavoured, crisp outside, soft inside, warm yellow and easy to make with readily-available ingredients.

What's in a name? Legend has it that when hunting dogs returned home with their masters after a day's sport, hungry and barking noisily, bits of fried cornmeal mixture were thrown at them for peace and quiet with the words "hush puppy". True or false, it's a nice story.

1 Tip cornmeal and flour into a bowl. Mix in onion, salt, pepper and baking powder then let mixture run through your fingers.

2 Stir in water and egg. Heat oil until hot, add heaped teaspoons of mixture and fry for about a minute or until well-puffed and golden.

3 Drain on kitchen paper towels and serve hot with fried fish.

Pain Perdu

6 slices medium thick white bread (you can use brown if you want to)
150ml (¼pt) creamy milk or single cream
2 grade 1 or 2 eggs
1 tsp vanilla essence
a large frying pan, one-third filled with corn oil
25g (1oz) icing sugar, sifted

This translates from the French into Lost Bread and equates to our Knights in Armour or French toast. In Louisiana, it is eaten by Cajuns for breakfast with grillades and grits (page 39). It is also thought of as a light supper dish and usually coated lightly with sugar, honey or syrup. Breadcrumbs apart, it's probably the nicest way of coping with stale bread.

1 *Trim crusts off bread then cut each slice into two triangles.*

2 *Beat together milk or cream, eggs, essence and vanilla.*

3 *Dip bread into milk mixture then brown on both sides in the oil.*

4 *Serve hot, dusted with sugar.*

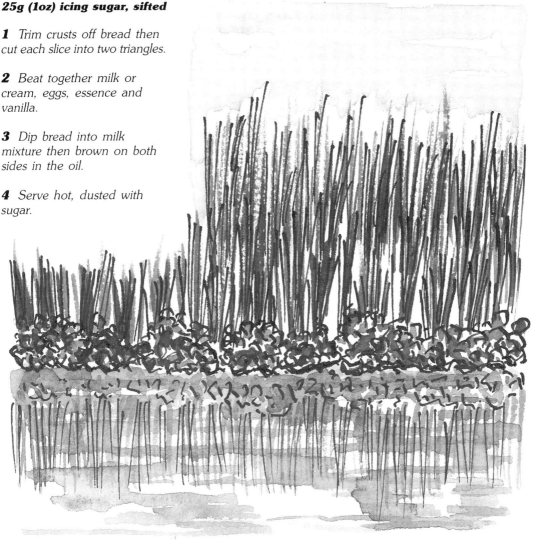

Spoon Bread

**150g (5oz) cornmeal
(polenta)
150g (5oz) plain flour
3 level tsp baking powder
1 level tsp salt
175ml (6 fluid oz) milk
40g (1½oz) butter or
margarine, melted
2 grade 2 eggs, beaten
2 slightly rounded tblsp
black treacle**

"Ugh", I thought to myself when I first read the recipe for this southern corn bread. "How can anyone eat treacly bread with bacon?" So I tried it and it was delicious, appropriate and even complementary. Farming communities make the bread when they join together to celebrate the slaughter of several hogs in one session which are then turned into French style Boucherie (butchery) products; head cheese, pâtés, Jambalaya, sausages, fiery jerky and crackling from rendered down pork skin. The cracklings sometimes go into the bread but I've spared you that one.

1 Thickly grease an oblong baking dish measuring 20 by 18cm (about 7 by 8 inches). Heat in oven set to 190°C (375°F), Gas 5.

2 Meanwhile, tip cornmeal into a bowl. Sift in flour, baking powder and salt.

3 Beat in rest of ingredients. Pour into hot tin and bake 20 to 25 minutes or until firm to the touch and golden.

4 Spoon on to plates and eat hot or warm.

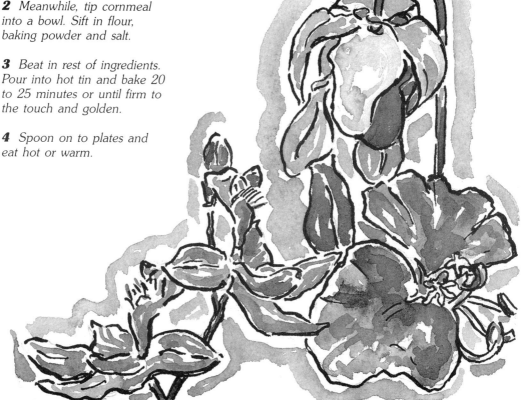

Cornbread

SERVES 4 TO 6

150g (5oz) cornmeal
(polenta)
150g (5oz) plain flour
1 level tblsp baking
powder
1 level tsp salt
2 level tblsp caster sugar
175ml (6 fluid oz) cold
milk
1 grade 1 egg, beaten
50g (2oz) butter or
margarine, melted

1 Well grease an 18 by
20cm (7 by 8 inch) roasting
tin. Set oven to 180°C
(350°F), Gas 4.

2 Tip cornmeal into a bowl.
Sift in flour, baking powder,
salt and sugar.

3 Beat together last 3
ingredients. Fork-stir into
cornmeal mixture to form a
softish mixture.

4 Transfer to prepared tin
and bake about 20 to 25
minutes or until fairly well-
risen and golden brown.

5 Remove from oven, cut
into squares and serve straight
away with butter or margarine.

*Golden squares of nourishment are what Cornbread's all
about; a slightly coarse-textured 'cake' which is cut up into
pieces and served with butter for breakfast or eaten later with
fried fish or fried chicken.*

Sweet Things

Fat Man's Misery

SERVES 8

**200g (7oz) chocolate
digestive biscuits, crushed
225g (8oz) butter, softened
to kitchen temperature
140g (4½oz) icing sugar,
sifted
1 grade 2 egg
1 tblsp milk
2 or 3 drops almond
essence
275ml (½pt) double cream,
whipped
1 rounded tblsp caster
sugar
1 tsp vanilla essence
125g (4oz) walnuts or
pecan nuts, fairly finely
chopped**

Sweat breaks out on the fat man's brow, he drools uncontrollably, his cheeks flush red and with lamentable lack of self-control he indulges in this fantasy of creamy riches, his pudgy fingers loosening the neck of his shirt and all feelings of guilt flung to the winds, his ecstasy complete.

I have found the Misery as far afield as Canada and California and this is my own adaptation based on a recipe straight from Louisiana.

1 Brush the inside of a fancy dish lightly with melted butter. It should be about 5cm (2 inches) deep with a top measurement of 20cm (8 inches) sloping to 18cm (7 inches) across the base.

2 Press a fairly thick layer of biscuits over base and sides of dish, reserving a third for the topping.

3 Beat butter and icing sugar until light, fluffy and very pale in colour. Beat in egg, milk and almond essence. Spread smoothly into dish to form a single layer. Refrigerate until firm.

4 Whip cream until thick then stir in caster sugar, vanilla essence and nuts. Spread over butter cream layer, cover thickly with rest of crumbs and press down lightly with the palm of your hand.

5 Refrigerate until firm. To serve, spoon out on to plates or cut into wedges if firm enough.

Consideration

If you dislike almond essence, use only vanilla.

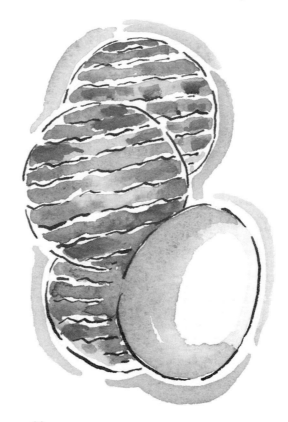

Sweet Potato Pudding

SERVES 8 TO 10

1kg (just over 2lb) sweet potatoes, peeled and diced
boiling water
125g (4oz) caster sugar or golden syrup
75g (3oz) butter or margarine, melted
2 grade 1 or 2 eggs, beaten
1 tsp vanilla essence
1 level tsp allspice

Topping
50g (2oz) butter or margarine, melted
125g (4oz) light brown soft sugar
50g (2oz) plain flour
25g (1oz) cornmeal (polenta)
125g (4oz) pecan nuts, fairly finely chopped

Lavish with crème fraîche or vanilla ice cream, the pudding is one I made up and I hope it meets with the approval of my friends in Louisiana. It uses sweet potatoes and pecans, both local crops, so isn't too far off the beaten track.

1 Put potatoes into a pan. Cover with boiling water and cook with lid on 15 to 20 minutes or until tender.

2 Drain and very finely mash or work to a purée in a blender goblet or food processor. Transfer to a bowl.

3 Beat in rest of ingredients and spread evenly into a greased dish measuring 28 by 23cm (11 by 9 inches).

4 Stir topping ingredients well together and sprinkle over pie.

5 Bake for 25 to 30 minutes in oven set to 180°C (350°F), Gas 4. Pudding is ready when topping is just beginning to turn golden.

6 Remove from oven and spoon on to plates. Serve warm.

Bread Pudding

SERVES 8 TO 12

275g (10oz) French bread, cut into small cubes
225g (8oz) caster sugar
125g (4oz) butter or margarine, melted
4 grade 2 eggs, beaten
575ml (1pt) milk, heated until lukewarm
350g (12oz) mixed dried fruit
1 tsp vanilla essence
1½ level tsp allspice or cinnamon
whisky sauce (page 72)

It's full of sweetness and light, soft as a down pillow, gentle, a Southern belle of a pudding laden with fruit and delicately spiced, appealing, wholesome, golden-topped, sumptuous with whisky sauce, a grand old-timer and a Louisiana institution. Irresistible — provided you don't count calories.

1 Well grease a tin measuring 28 by 20cm (11 by 8 inches). Set oven to 180°C (350°F), Gas 4.

2 Tip bread cubes into a mixing bowl. Add all remaining ingredients, stir well and leave to stand about 10 minutes until bread softens.

3 Transfer to prepared dish and bake for 1 hour when pudding should be puffy and top golden.

4 Spoon out on to plates and serve hot with whisky sauce.

Consideration

Leftovers can be eaten cold or individual portions reheated for a few seconds in the microwave.

Bananas Foster

50g (2oz) butter (no, not margarine, thank you)
8 large bananas, peeled
50g (2oz) soft dark brown sugar
½ level tsp cinnamon
2 tblsp Grand Marnier
150ml (¼pt) dark rum
whipped cream for serving

1 Melt butter in a large frying pan. Add bananas and fry gently until golden, turning carefully with 2 spoons.

Foster, please come forward and identify yourself! I can't find reference to you anywhere; not in any book, not in any article, pamphlet, leaflet, booklet. Why are you associated with bananas? What makes you so desirable? Where are you hiding? Somebody must know.

2 Add sugar, cinnamon and Grand Marnier. Continue to heat, turning bananas over once. Transfer to a warm serving dish.

3 Separately, heat rum until lukewarm. Flame with a match and pour over the bananas. Serve with thick whipped cream.

Consideration

If you have it available, use banana liqueur instead of the Grand Marnier.

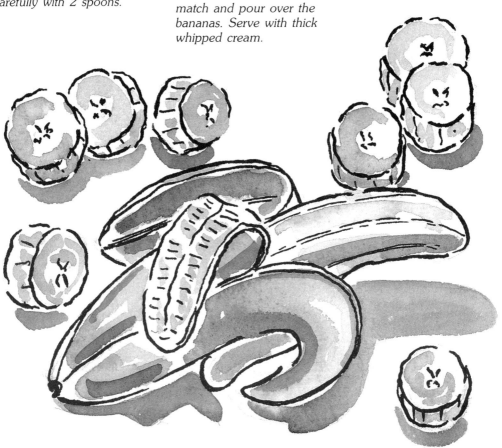

Creole 'Cream Cheese' Ice Cream

SERVES 6 TO 8

200g (7oz) crème fraîche, shop bought in a tub or homemade
575ml (1pt) cold and lightly sweetened custard, bought or homemade and flavoured with vanilla
4 slightly rounded tblsp caster sugar

1 Beat together all the ingredients.

2 Transfer to a bowl, cover with foil and freeze until there is a solid border of about 5cm (2 inches) round inside of bowl.

3 Beat until creamy, cover and re-freeze until firm.

Whole books have been written about ice cream in the USA and in a recent mail order food magazine, there were 51 ways of dressing up shop bought ice cream with additions ranging from fried apple rings with sugar to a sprinkling of espresso coffee powder over scoops of chocolate chip.

I suppose one could say ice cream in Louisiana is more restrained though I must admit I haven't eaten my way through a fraction of all those on offer.

Cream cheese ice cream sounds off-putting but my dear friend Yves, Chef at London's 51 51 restaurant, explained that the cream cheese bit actually meant crème fraîche, that rich and slightly soured cream so beloved in France for general culinary purposes. And in Louisiana too, it seems.

Crème Fraîche can be problematic to find outside London so I have developed a recipe of my own which is on page 114. It is almost identical with the real thing and is less expensive.

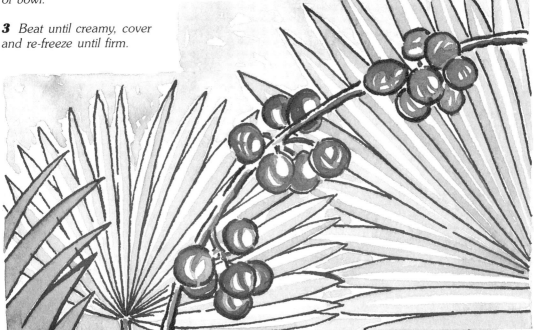

Vanilla Ice Cream

**150g (5oz) double cream
142ml carton Crème
Fraîche or 150g (5oz)
homemade
575ml (1pt) cold and
lightly sweetened custard,
bought or homemade
3 rounded tblsp caster
sugar
1½ tsp vanilla essence**

Also Louisiana in temperament, this is a smoother, lighter textured and creamier version of the 'Cream Cheese' ice cream. It is the true classic for the Mississippi Mud Pie (page 98).

1 Whip cream until thick and combine with the Crème Fraîche.

2 Using a large spoon, work in custard, sugar and essence.

3 Transfer to a bowl, cover with foil and freeze until there is a solid border of about 5cm (2 inches) round inside of bowl.

4 Beat until creamy, cover and re-freeze until firm.

Caramel Ice Cream

225g (8oz) fudge
3 tblsp milk
150g (5oz) double cream
575ml (1pt) cold and
lightly sweetened custard,
bought or homemade

The favourite ingredient for Louisiana Mud Pie, I have simplified the recipe by taking one of my shortcuts which are now legion – using ready-prepared fudge instead of making caramel which is tricky and time-consuming. Use only top quality fudge. Anything less and the taste is marred completely.

1 Put fudge into saucepan with milk and melt over a low heat, stirring constantly. Remove from heat and cool to lukewarm.

2 Beat cream until thick and combine smoothly with custard. Gently work in melted fudge.

3 Transfer to a bowl, cover with foil and freeze until there is a solid border of about 5cm (2 inches) round inside of bowl.

4 Beat until creamy, cover and re-freeze until firm.

Chocolate Ice Cream

**100g (3½oz) plain chocolate
150g (5oz) double cream
142ml carton Crème Fraîche or 150g (5oz) homemade (page 114)
575ml (1pt) cold and lightly sweetened custard
1 tsp vanilla essence
2 rounded tblsp caster sugar**

The all-time best-thing-to-have-happened-in-the-world since sliced bread. A classy ice cream for every reason, every season, glamorous, voluptuous and another ingredient for the Mississippi Mud Pie. No wonder it's so sought after.

1 Break up chocolate and melt in a basin over a pan of hot water or at defrost setting in the microwave, allowing about 3 to 3½ minutes.

2 Remove basin from saucepan or microwave and stir chocolate until smooth.

3 Beat double cream until thick and combine smoothly with Crème Fraîche, custard, essence and sugar.

4 Add to chocolate, spoon by spoon. Whip gently until well combined.

5 Transfer to a bowl, cover with foil and freeze until there is a solid border of about 5cm (2 inches) round inside of bowl.

6 Beat until creamy, cover and re-freeze until firm.

Sweet Potato Pie

Shortcrust pastry made with 175g (6oz) flour and 75 to 100g (3 – 3½oz) fat (page 116)

Filling

**450g (1lb) sweet potatoes, peeled and cubed
boiling water
75g (3oz) soft light brown sugar
2 level tsp mixed spice
3 grade 2 eggs, beaten
150ml (¼pt) milk
25g (1oz) butter or margarine, melted**

Silken smooth and made from one of Louisiana's local crops, Sweet Potatoe Pie is easy to copy now that the potatoes are readily available in the U.K. They tend to be elongated with pinky skins and yellow insides, not to be confused with yams which are brown outside, cream within and totally different in taste and texture.

1 Roll out pastry and use to line a 20cm (8 inch) flan dish. Line with foil to prevent pastry from rising as it cooks. Bake 20 minutes in oven set to 220°C (425°F), Gas 7. Reduce temperature to 180°C (350°F), Gas 4.

2 Meanwhile, simmer potatoes in enough boiling water to cover. Add lid. They should tenderise in 15 to 20 minutes. Drain and very finely mash or work to a purée in a blender goblet or food processor. Transfer to a bowl.

3 Beat in all remaining ingredients. Remove pastry from oven and lift out foil. Pour in the potato mixture and bake for a further 30 to 40 minutes or until filling is set. Serve just cold with cream or vanilla ice cream.

Consideration

All filling ingredients may be blended together in a food processor until they form a smooth purée.

Pies

All North Americans are devoted to pies and hold them in the highest possible esteem. You don't fool with a pie. Some of the classics are pecan, sweet potato and Mississippi Mud which is fast catching on over here as the "in" thing to be seen with. All have been included.

Yves' Mississippi Mud Pie

SERVES 8 TO 10

Shortcrust pastry (page 116) made with 225g (8oz) plain flour PLUS 25g (1oz) caster sugar added to sifted ingredients
chocolate ice cream (page 96)
vanilla ice cream (page 94)
or
Creole cream cheese ice cream (page 93)

Meringue

3 grade 3 egg whites
pinch of salt
175g (6oz) caster sugar

1 Roll out pastry and use to line a 23cm (9 inch) fluted flan dish. Press a piece of foil over base and sides to prevent pastry from rising as it cooks.

2 Bake 20 minutes in oven set to 220°C (425°F), Gas 7. Remove foil and continue to bake for a further 10 minutes or so when pastry should be a light golden brown. Cool completely.

3 To finish, fill with scoops of chocolate ice cream topped with the vanilla or Creole cream cheese ice cream. Freeze while making meringue. Set oven to 230°C (450°F), Gas 8.

4 Whip whites and salt to a stiff snow. Gradually beat in sugar and continue to beat until meringue is shiny and stands in firm peaks.

Yves is a great character, a super chef based at London's Cajun 51-51 restaurant and knows New Orleans cooking like the back of his hand. Get him on the subject of Cajun/Creole food and he grins broadly, white teeth gleam in his lovely black face, eyes sparkle and there he is, off like a Derby Winner, trying to tell you his life time culinary background over a two hour lunch. Quite an education!

His interpretation of the MMP is below and is a dream come true.

5 Swirl over pie and flash 5 minutes in the oven until meringue is tipped with gold but ice cream is still firm. Cut into wedges and serve straight away.

Double Chocolate Mississippi Mud Pie

SERVES 8 TO 10

Make the pastry case with "chocolate" pastry by substituting 1 level tablespoon cocoa powder (sifted) for the same amount of flour. Increase fat by 15g (½oz).

Mississippi Mud Pie

Named after the Bayou areas in Louisiana, Mississippi Mud Pie has taken off like a rocket and recipes for it are rapidly appearing all over the place as enthusiasm for Cajun and Creole food intensifies by the minute. You must have noticed it if you're into innovative eating experiences.

Devastatingly Decadent Mississippi Mud Pie

SERVES 8 TO 10

Forget the meringue or cream. Top pie with trickles of warm chocolate sauce made by melting 100g (3½oz) plain chocolate then stirring in 4 tblsp double cream and one of any liqueur you fancy – or none at all.

Louisiana Mississippi Mud Pie

SERVES 8 TO 10

Another one from Yves.
Make as first pie, substituting caramel ice cream for the vanilla.

Creamy Mississippi Mud Pie

SERVES 8 TO 10

Instead of meringue, top pie with a cloud of softly whipped and lightly sweetened cream.

Coconut Pie

SERVES 10

Pie Shell
Shortcrust pastry made with 225g (8oz) plain flour, 125g (4oz) fat and water to bind (page 116)

Filling
**5 grade 1 eggs
125g (4oz) butter or margarine, melted
150 (¼pt) buttermilk (page 114)
350g (12oz) caster sugar
1 tsp vanilla
150g (5oz) desiccated coconut**

I apologise for possibly spoiling your appetite but this beauty of a pie is served at Catholic wakes when families join together to mourn their dead. The occasion is always a social one, a time for exchanging family news, meeting old friends and catching up on gossip.

The object is to keep the body company until the burial and it shows a spirit of goodwill and kindness matched with genuine sympathy. Food at these times is always plentiful, often sweet and cakes and pies are baked in abundance for the send-off. In my opinion, this is one of the nicest.

1 *Set oven to 220°C (425°F), Gas 7. Roll out pastry and use to line a 25cm (10 inch) greased flan dish, plain or fluted. Line with foil to prevent pastry from rising as it cooks.*

2 *Bake 20 minutes, carefully remove foil and bake another 10 minutes or until pastry is golden. Remove from oven. Reduce temperature to 180°C (350°F) Gas 4.*

3 *Beat all filling ingredients well together. Pour into pie shell and bake about 45 minutes or until filling has set and feels firm to the touch. Leave to finish off for 15 minutes in the oven with the heat switched off and door ajar.*

4 *Remove from oven and leave until just cold before cutting into portions and serving. Store leftovers in the refrigerator and warm through slightly before eating.*

Buttermilk Pie

SERVES 10

**4 grade 2 eggs
275ml (½pt) buttermilk
(page 114)
350g (12oz) caster sugar
1 tsp vanilla essence
125g (4oz) butter or
margarine, melted**

Less rich than Custard pie, this one is a gem to have on hand after a spicy meal. It soothes and pacifies with immense subtlety and a little goes a long way.

Make exactly as the Coconut Pie (page 99) but use the following filling:

Pecan Pie

SERVES 8 TO 10

Shortcrust pastry made with 225g (8oz) flour and 125g (4oz) fat plus water to mix (page 116). Or 350g (12oz) readymade pastry.

Filling

**200g (7oz) pecan nuts, lightly toasted
25g (1oz) butter or margarine, melted
225g (8oz) caster sugar
225g (8oz) golden syrup, melted
3 grade 2 eggs, well-beaten
1 tsp vanilla essence**

A real sweetheart of a pie and the most popular belle down South where the pecans grow. It is a distant relation of treacle tart and just as sweet.

1 *Roll out pastry and use to line a 25cm (10 inch) fluted flan tin or dish. Spread pecans over base.*

2 *Beat rest of ingredients well together and pour into flan over nuts.*

3 *Bake 45 minutes in oven set 190°C (375°F), Gas 5. Leave until lukewarm then cut into wedges. Serve with softly whipped cream.*

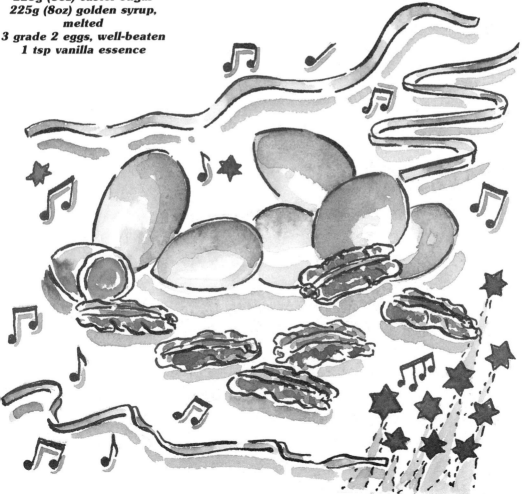

Pralines

**125g (4oz) pecans, lightly
toasted and coarsely
chopped
1 can (400g or 14oz)
sweetened condensed milk
175g (6oz) dark brown soft
sugar
150ml (¼pt) milk
75g (3oz) butter
1 tsp vanilla essence**

Are they cookies (biscuits) or are they candies (sweets)? Books vary but pralines are part and parcel of Louisiana and every inch the lady − well-rounded and always presentable.

Large pralines can be served for tea alongside other cakes. Little ones are fine to offer with coffee after a meal instead of mint chocs.

They are difficult to describe exactly but I would class them as softish fudge, full of pecans and extremely sweet.

1 *Cover two or three chopping boards with non-stick parchment paper.*

2 *Put all ingredients except the essence into a heavy-based pan and bring to the boil, stirring constantly with a wooden spoon.*

3 *Continue to boil for about 15 to 20 minutes or until a little of the mixture, when dropped into a cup of cold water, can be shaped into a soft ball between finger and thumb. (Temperature on sugar thermometer should be 116°C or 240°F). Stir frequently.*

4 *Remove from heat and stir in vanilla. Cool for 10 minutes then stand pan of praline mixture in a sink with some cold water in it (NOT an enamel sink which could crack).*

5 *Start beating steadily and continue until mixture thickens up, loses its gloss almost completely and looks creamy.*

6 *Spoon into rounds on the paper-covered boards and leave until cold. Turn over so that undersides have a chance to dry out.*

7 *When firm (I leave mine out overnight covered with paper), pack into a tin or box with tissue paper between each layer.*

Beignets

SERVES 3 TO 4

choux pastry to make 12:
65g (2½oz) plain flour
150ml (¼pt) water
50g (2oz) unsalted butter
1 tsp vanilla essence
2 grade 2 or 3 eggs, well-beaten
a pan of deep oil for frying
sifted icing sugar for sprinkling

Beignets are crisp, golden puff balls of fried lightness submerged beneath an avalanche of icing sugar and served with steaming cups of café au lait, freshly-breshly and tasting of heaven. I remember eating them, mid-morning, in a café in the French quarter of New Orleans, listening to the steady beat of rhythm and blues provided by a local group of musicians who joined forces for an impromptu jam session. Such entertainment!

1 Sift flour into a bowl.

2 Heat water and butter slowly together until butter melts then bring to a brisk boil.

3 Shoot in flour in one go, add vanilla and stir briskly until mixture thickens, makes its way towards centre of pan and leaves sides clean.

4 Now think you are making mayonnaise and try to borrow a third hand.

5 Beat in eggs, drop by drop, until mixture is smooth, glossy and stands in peaks when lifted up with a spoon.

6 Heat oil until hot. Drop in dessertspoons of mixture and fry until they puff out and turn light gold. They will float to the top of the oil and it's a good idea to turn them over so that they cook evenly.

7 Drain on crumpled kitchen paper and coat with icing sugar.

Ambrosia

**6 medium oranges (750g
or 1¾lb)
1 can (432g or 15½oz)
pineapple pieces
1 jar (125g or 4oz)
maraschino cocktail
cherries (red)
50g (2oz) desiccated
coconut**

*Fit for the Christmas or Mardi Gras Gods − a mix of fruits
and coconut with maraschino cherries. It needs overnight
chilling and each portion should be dolloped with a mound of
soured cream or Crème Fraîche (page 114).*

1 *Peel oranges, remove all
traces of pith and slice thinly.
Transfer to a mixing bowl.*

2 *Add remaining ingredients.
Toss gently to mix. Cover
and refrigerate overnight.*

La Cuite

*A curious, old-fashioned
mixture served as a dessert.
It consists of thick syrup
(I use golden) with lightly
toasted and chopped
pecans folded in. It's mur-
derously sweet and the
only way to tone it down
is with whipped cream on
every portion.*

*Allow about 2 table-
spoons per person.*

Divinity

MAKES 20 OR 40

non-stick parchment
paper or foil
450g (1lb) caster sugar
125g (4oz) golden syrup
150ml (¼pt) hot water
2 egg whites from
grade 2 eggs
2 pinches of salt
2 tsp vanilla essence
125g (4oz) pecan nuts,
coarsely chopped
20 glacé cherries

The angels sing more sweetly in the South, hence Divinity. They are what the Americans call candy, sweets over here, and look like puff balls of clouds with gentle peaks; even fresh white snowballs or creamy meringues. Chopped pecans fill their entire world and cherries on top make a bright and jazzy contribution to the overall charm. I love them, but then I love everything sweet. The texture is soft, sensual and almost like marshmallow and the whole idea is to serve them alone, as sweets or cakes, partnered with coffee or, when small enough, as petit fours at the end of a meal. They take a bit of doing and you will need a fairly powerful set of electric beaters – don't even try by hand.

1 Line a large tray with parchment or foil. Leave on one side for the time being.

2 Tip sugar into a saucepan with a heavyish base. Add syrup and water.

3 Bring to boil slowly over a moderate heat. Stir often.

4 Increase heat and boil fairly briskly for about 15 to 18 minutes. Syrup is hot enough when a small amount forms a hardish but pliable ball when dropped from a teaspoon into a cup of cold water. (If using a confectionery thermometer, the temperature should be no less than 120°C or 250°F). Remove pan from heat.

5 In a large bowl, beat egg whites stiffly with salt. With care and hands protected by oven gloves, pour the hot syrup into the beaten whites in a slow, steady stream.

6 Continue to beat until mixture is almost cold and begins to feel heavy. By now it should be quite peaky and much paler in colour than when you started.

7 I can't give an exact time for this process but you should recognise the signs. Stop the beaters then stir in essence and pecans.

8 Spoon out 20 heaps of mixture on to lined trays then top each with a cherry.

9 Leave overnight in a cool, DRY place. Store airtight with tissue paper between the layers.

LITTLE DIVINITIES FOR PETIT FOURS

Divide into 40 heaps and top each with half a glacé cherry. Put into small paper cases.

105

Drinks

Café au Lait

Go to the French quarter when you're next in New Orleans, settle down inside or outside any café and ask for café au lait. Then make it when you get home like this:

With a jug of hot milk in one hand and a jug of freshly brewed filter coffee in the other, pour equal amounts of both simultaneously into cups. Sweeten to taste, or not.

Consideration

It's the customary mid-morning drink in Louisiana and loved by children.

Coffee and Chicory

Coffee flavoured with chicory, completely in French style, is the most favoured type in Louisiana. It is served very strong and black and is used for iced coffee.

Café Brûlot

SERVES 6

A heady, aromatic brew for dark winter evenings and grown-up parties.

peel of 1 washed and dried orange, in a continuous strip
finely grated peel of 1 washed and dried lemon
6 cloves
10 sugar cubes
½ a cinnamon stick
125ml (4 fluid oz) brandy
125ml (4 fluid oz) Grand Marnier
275ml (½pt) strong black coffee (filter type)

1 Put orange and lemon peels into fondue type pot or chafing dish.

2 Add cloves, sugar, cinnamon and a splash of brandy. Heat slowly until warm and sugar begins to melt.

3 Add rest of brandy and Grand Marnier. Heat until hot then set alight.

4 Slowly add coffee and pour into handled demi-tasse cups. Drink hot.

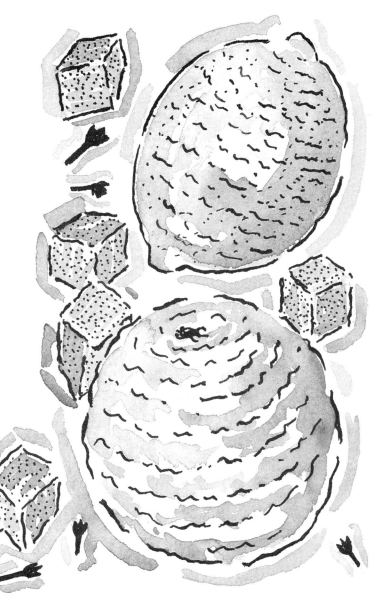

Cyclone

SERVES 1

A sensual mix with an unexpected piquancy.

**50ml (2 fluid oz) vodka
25ml (1 fluid oz) passion
fruit syrup (or mango juice
if easier to find)
25ml (1 fluid oz) fresh
lemon juice
crushed ice
1 slice of orange
1 maraschino cherry**

1 Shake together first 3
ingredients.

2 Pour into a glass, half-
filled with crushed ice.

3 Decorate with orange slice
and cherry on a stick.

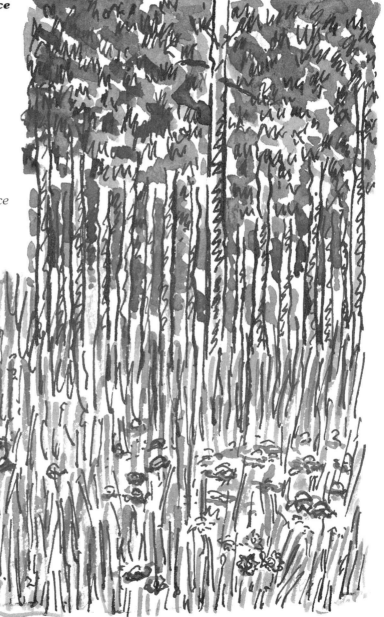

Pina Colada

SERVES 1

A zingy cocktail with a taste of intrigue. Full of exoticism.

50g (2oz) cream of coconut (available in packets from many supermarket chains), melted over hot water
125ml (4 fluid oz) pineapple juice
25ml (1 fluid oz) white rum
6 ice cubes
2 maraschino cherries

1 Put first 3 ingredients into a blender goblet.

2 Add 4 ice cubes. Run blender until drink is frothy and ice fairly well crushed.

3 Pour into a glass. Add remaining ice cubes then decorate with cherries on a stick, even fingers or wedges of fresh pineapple.

Mint Julep

SERVES 1

Simple Syrup
175g (6oz) caster sugar
150ml (¼pt) water

Cool as ice, gently sweet, delicately fragrant and one of the nicer ways of using Bourbon – North America's deep gold whisky. Lest you have none, substitute Irish with an "e".

1 Put both into a pan and heat gently until sugar dissolves. Leave until cold.

For the Julep
4 sprigs of mint
75ml (3 fluid oz) Bourbon
1 tblsp syrup as above
crushed ice

1 Crush 3 mint sprigs in a medium tumbler – the best way is with the back of a teaspoon.

2 Add Bourbon and syrup then fill glass with crushed ice. Float in remaining mint.

Bloody Mary

SERVES 1

crushed ice
50ml (2 fluid oz) vodka
1 tsp lime juice cordial
¼ tsp Worcester sauce
2 shakes Tabasco
125ml (4 fluid oz) tomato
juice
2 pinches of salt
slice of lime to decorate

1 Half fill glass with ice.

2 Add next 6 ingredients.
Stir well to mix.

3 Decorate with slice of
lime.

A hot contribution to the list of cold cocktails with a slight twist from me via the lime.

Lagniappe

Lagniappe

Andouille
A spicy sausage much used in Louisiana cooking. It is pure pork and smoked. The nearest equivalents are Spanish Chorizo or Polish salami.

This word means a little something extra – an idea, notion, afterthought, hint, tip, food, drink, cooking term, happiness serendipity.

Buttermilk
On sale spasmodically and only in selected retail outlets, the National Dairy Council worked out this compromise for me some years ago and I have been making it ever since.

Combine equal quantities of natural, unflavoured yogurt with skimmed or semi-skimmed milk. Whisk gently until smooth then use as required.

Crème Fraîche
The all-purpose French cream for cooking and some selected desserts. It's findable from time to time over here from supermarkets but I prefer to make my own and have it on the spot. And it's the easiest thing in the world to do.

Combine equal quantities of soured and double cream. Whisk gently together in a bowl. Cover and leave over-night in the kitchen during winter, about 6 hours in summer. It's ready when you

lift out a spoonful and the mixture has obviously thicken-ed. It should also taste slightly lactic, like Danish butter. Keep covered and refrigerate up to a week.

Etouffée of Beef
Translated the étouffée bit means smothered and refers to any food immersed in gravy – rather like the French estouffade. It is identical with the Beef Daube on page 41.

Blackened Chicken
Cook the same way as the blackened red fish (page 30). Beat chicken breasts until flat, dip in butter and coat with seasoning. Allow a little longer time – about ½–1 minute per side.

Roux
A roux is a mixture of plain flour with oil or melted fat (butter, margarine, dripping or bacon fat) in equal quantities. *It is used to thicken sauces, soups and gravies and also add to the flavour of the liquid. The New Orleans Creole dishes are usually based on a light roux in line with French haute cuisine. The Acadians or Cajuns prefer it to be darker to match their robust and rustic style of cooking.*

To make, heat oil or melt fat in a pan. For a light roux, add flour and cook for 1 minute, stirring. For a dark roux, continue to cook until the mixture turns gingersnap tan or the colour of a walnut shell; about 3 to 4 minutes. Stir constantly and take off heat quickly once the roux has darkened. If it continues to cook, it will burn quickly and become unusable.

Tasso

Cajuns cook strong and Tasso is a simple example. It is a form of highly-seasoned Jerky, made from strips of dried pork impregnated with Cajun seasoning (page 118). The seasoning blend varies from cook to cook but whoever makes it ensures it has a potent enough taste to add a distinctive flavour to Jambalaya, Gumbo, any kind of stew and soups. Unless you have a smokehouse, it is almost impossible to make at home and one reasonable compromise is to cut top smoked gammon into tiny cubes and coat with the seasoning where it will keep up to a week or so in the refrigerator.

The Trinity

A term used by Joe Cahn, from the New Orleans School of Cooking, to describe the three vegetables which are used together in many of Louisiana's savoury dishes: green peppers (known in the USA as bell peppers), onions and celery.

Chicken Sauce Piquante

Make sauce exactly as for alligator (page 48). After bringing to the boil (point 3) add 4 chicken portions. Cover and simmer for 45 minutes or until bird is tender. Serve as the alligator.

Rabbit Sauce Piquante

Make sauce exactly as for alligator (page 48). After bringing to the boil (point 3) add 1 medium sized rabbit, jointed and soaked in lemon juice and water for 3 hours. Cover and simmer for 45 minutes to 1 hour or until rabbit meat is tender. Serve as the alligator.

Aubergine Casserole

SERVES 4 TO 6

Make as Aubergine Casserole with Beef (page 38) but omit beef. Serve as a side dish with roast poultry or as a main meal with fried mushrooms and tomatoes.

Shortcrust Pastry

**225g (8oz) plain flour
pinch of salt
125g (4oz) butter,
margarine or white
vegetable cooking fat
about 4 tblsp cold water
for mixing**

Known in the USA as pie crust, this equates to our own short-crust pastry with the same ratio of ingredients.

1 Sift flour and salt into a bowl.

2 Add one choice of fat or mixture of fats, cut into flour with a round-tipped knife then rub in finely with finger tips.

3 Add water in one go then stir into pastry until it forms large crumbs.

4 Draw together with finger tips, knead lightly until smooth then roll out and use as required.

Batter for cooking fried foods

125g (4oz) flour (see right)
pinch of salt
1 grade 3 egg
150ml (¼pt) milk

A standard batter which is very good for coating food to be deep fried. If you want it to puff-up a bit, use half plain flour and half self-raising. To make it even more light and crispy, use the amount of milk below minus 2 tablespoons then fold in one stiffly beaten egg white.

1 Sift flour and salt into a bowl.

2 Beat in egg and milk to form a thick and creamy batter. Cover and refrigerate for about 1 hour.

3 Stir round before using to ensure smoothness.

Cajun Seasoning

15g (½oz) salt
15g (½oz) garlic salt
25g (1oz) white pepper
25g (1oz) black pepper
25g (1oz) cayenne pepper
25g (1oz) poultry seasoning
25g (1oz) dried oregano
25g (1oz) dried basil
25g (1oz) dried cumin

1 To prevent sneezing because of pepper, wear a face mask which most pharmacies keep in stock.

2 Put first 6 ingredients into a bowl or basin.

3 In a small electric processor or grinder, work last 3 herbs to a powder. Or use a pestle and mortar if you prefer.

4 Combine with first mixture and keep in a well-stoppered jar. A dark cupboard is the best place for storage.

Mr J C Autin produces a fine-smelling seasoning for Cajun dishes which is available from speciality food shops and the inevitable Harrods. I bought my jar of 151g/15.3oz for £2.55 and I was desperately trying to work out my own formula for the sake of economy. Being at best a moderate cook with inspirational flashes now and again, and at worst an impatient one with minimal time for exploratory shopping expeditions, I am very grateful indeed to Executive Chef Ed Keeling, of the Hyatt Regency in New Orleans, for passing on a spice mix which he uses for blackened fish dishes (page 30). To my way of thinking, the mix is all-purpose and can be added to anything from soups to stews, gumbos, rice, Jambalay's, even scrambled eggs. But it's a red hot Momma with fury and to make it viable for virgin palates I have toned it down by using half the amount of cayenne pepper recommended. Also, to match up a bit with Autin's, garlic salt has been included. Use ¼ level tsp seasoning for every 4 servings.

'Po-Boys'

No-one could describe 'Po-Boys' (Poor Boys) better than Bobby Potts in his book on French Acadian Cooking.

"A lunch of 'Po-Boys' is as traditional in the Gulf Coast areas as any old custom existing. A 'Po-Boy' was considered the cheapest lunch possible – just a huge sandwich of French bread which could be copiously filled with anything from ham and cheese or chicken to meat balls or fried oysters. They are not so cheap today, but they have always been consumed by rich and poor alike. They are a challenge, for the possibilities are endless.

A 'Po-Boy' sandwich is made up of an entire small loaf of French bread, or about ¼ of one of the extremely long loaves of French bread, sliced lengthwise into a top and a bottom. It is then spread with mayonnaise, butter or any other spread and topped with mustard (preferably hot), ketchup or any other dressing or sauce that seems to go well with the contents. Almost any Louisianian will then add a lot of hot sauce. Lettuce is usually a basic ingredient. Ham, cheese, tomatoes and sliced onions are probably the most common filling, but the range is unbounded. It can be a meal or a salad in itself. Barbecued meat, roast beef, cooked seafood, fried seafood (shrimp, crawfish and oysters), meat loaf, fried catfish fillets, meat balls or any combination of the above are used. One enterprising restaurant cuts one end off a small loaf, pulls some of the soft innards out, and stuffs it with meatballs and tomato gravy. The soft inside absorbs the gravy well and the heavy crust keeps it from leaking through to the outside. The fried oyster 'Po-Boy' has been nicknamed the Peacemaker in New Orleans because a late arriving husband can placate his wife by bringing one home to her. Salami, bologna, pastrami and corned beef are also excellent 'stuffings'. A hot dog and chilli combination is often used, as are chicken salad and meat salads of all variety. Even fried eggs and bacon can be found layered between pieces of French bread. So, go and do your own thing!"

Foot Longs

Another name for 'Po-Boys', seen in New York.

Notes

Notes

Notes

Notes

Cast in no order of appearance

First—You make a Roux.
Published in 1954 by Les Vingt Quatre Club for Lafayette Museum.

Favourite New Orleans Recipes by Ormond, Irvine and Cantin. Published 1983 by Pelican Publishing Company.

Favourite Recipes from Famous New Orleans Restaurants. Distributed by Express Publishing Co. Inc., New Orleans (no date).

Cookin' on the Mississippi by Mrs Bobby Potts. Distributed by Express Publishing Co. Inc., New Orleans (no date).

The Shadows-on-The-Teche Cookbook. Published in 1982 by the Shadows Service League of New Iberia, Louisiana.

The Good Housekeeping Cookbook, Edited by Zoe Coulson. Published in 1973 by Good Housekeeping Books, New York, USA.

White Trash Cooking by Ernest Matthew Mickler. Published in 1985 by Ten Speed Press, USA.

Cotton Country Collection by the Junior Charity League of Monroe, Louisiana, first published in 1972.

Talk about Good 11, by the Junior League of Lafayette Inc., Lafayette, Louisiana, published in 1979.

French Acadian Cooking by Mrs Bobby Potts. Distributed by Express Publishing Co. Inc., New Orleans.

The Prudhomme Family Cookbook by the Eleven Prudhomme Brothers and Sisters and Chef Paul Prudhomme. Published in 1987 by William Morrow and Co. Inc., New York.

Chef Paul Prudhomme's Louisiana Kitchen. Published in 1984 by William Morrow and Co. Inc., New York.

Patout's Cajun Home Cooking by Alex Patout. Published in 1986 by Rondom House, New York, USA.

The Joy of Cooking by Rombauer and Becker. First published in 1931 by Bobbs-Merrill Co., Inc and in England by J. M. Dent and Sons Ltd.

The American Heritage Cookbook by the Editors of American Heritage, The Magazine of History. First published in paperback in 1967 by Penguin Books.

Antoine's Restaurant Cookbook by Roy F. Guste, Jr. Published in 1979 by Corbery-Guste, New Orleans.

Sonia Allison's Home Baking Book. Published in 1983 by David and Charles, Newton Abbot, England.

Plats du Jour by P Gray and P Boyd. Published in paperback in 1957 by Penguin Books.

Index